Contents

List of tables

Foreword

The way that decisions are made about who lives in social housing is changing rapidly. The impact of new Government agendas will be that over the next few years, lettings polices operated by local authorities and housing associations will become a patchwork of different practices.

For Shelter, and other organisations trying to strategically plan how housing needs are met, this has huge implications. We believe that it is vital that people who cannot afford or sustain the cost of renting or buying a home through the market are given access to subsidised housing that can provide long term stability. Affordable housing enables people to find work, develop their potential and raise and educate their children. The consequences of denying people in housing need access to local authority and housing association secure tenancies are severe. The impact will fall not only on individuals, but also will undermine the success of broader policies to tackle poverty and social exclusion. For these reasons, lettings policies matter.

But lettings policies are not just about allocating according to need. They also take account of the impact on neighbourhoods. There is a tension in practice between policies that aim to stabilise neighbourhoods by controlling access to housing, and providing housing for people in the greatest need. Understanding how this conflict affects people's housing options is vital. It is key to the development, both locally and nationally, of new agendas and policies on housing and neighbourhood renewal.

Central to the changing policy agenda is a new focus on choice for customers of local authorities and housing associations. How this develops in practice, through various local initiatives, will add a new dimension to the conflict between the needs of the individual and the needs of community.

The research published in this report was carried out before the publication of the Government's Housing Green Paper in April 2000. At the time of printing, the future of the Green Paper's homelessness proposals is uncertain. Whatever happens, the challenge will be to creatively integrate what is positive in old and new approaches, to develop a new agenda for the future. The message of this report is clear: the only way competing tensions can be reconciled to work at a local level is if the right information is collected and monitored. This report sets out what social landlords are doing now, and from this, we can all begin to move forward.

This report has been produced with thanks to the Nationwide Building Society.

Chris Holmes, *Director*, Shelter, June 2001

Summary

The policy debate

Social housing should be allocated to people in housing need, and lettings policies should be designed to give them housing priority. For many years that has been the consensus view among policy makers and housing professionals. In the 1990s, however, arguments began to be put forward that social landlords' lettings policies should contribute to other social objectives. It was argued that they should promote more choice, develop a more customer-focused approach and build 'sustainable' or 'balanced' communities.

In the 1990s the image of social housing became more and more negative. Some social landlords faced low demand for their homes. Some estates faced serious problems with crime and anti-social behaviour. Poverty became increasingly concentrated on some social housing estates. While these problems had a range of causes, the perception grew that allocations policies were largely to blame. The search intensified for new approaches.

As a result, many social landlords have, particularly since the Housing Act 1996, sought to develop lettings policies to address these diverse issues. They have sought to broaden access to social housing by letting to applicants from groups other than those in the greatest need, and, sometimes simultaneously, to restrict access by excluding households from the housing register who are seen to bring problems to the area. There is an inevitable tension within the lettings process between addressing need, promoting flexibility and customer choice, and achieving sustainable local communities.

Clear messages are emerging from the Government as to what lettings policy and practice should be aiming to achieve. These have been articulated in 'The way forward for housing' (DETR/DSS, 2000c) and underpinned the policy aims of the Homes Bill. The emphasis is on developing viable and sustainable communities, avoiding concentrations of particular types of household and promoting choice for all housing applicants. Alongside the Government's support for these objectives, draft guidance has been explicit about the importance of meeting the needs of homeless people. In practice, these aims may pull landlord action in different directions.

This research highlights examples of policies which, while delivering one objective, undermine other Government policy directions. For example, local exclusions from waiting lists on the basis of a criminal conviction would undermine the Government's intention to extend priority need to vulnerable people coming out of institutions who are homeless. In addition, policies to suspend or exclude from the housing register applicants who refuse a specified number of reasonable offers run counter to explicit statements in the Housing Green Paper that applicants should not be penalised for refusing offers. In a wider sense, they also undermine the promotion of opportunity and choice, which are key principles in the Government's vision of letting social housing in the future.

Much of the debate about new approaches to letting social housing has arisen from a need to find new ways to revive unpopular or low-demand housing and help create or sustain strong communities. This makes this agenda central to new attempts to tackle area disadvantage and to the developing work of the Neighbourhood Renewal Unit.

The fact that in many cases solutions to neighbourhood problems address the problems surrounding unpopular social housing while appearing to ignore the continuing presence of urgent housing need is of serious concern. Indeed, it is often the same people with urgent housing needs who are thought to contribute to making a neighbourhood unpopular. On this basis, failing to address these needs may simply move the 'problem' elsewhere. The lack of a definition of what constitutes a sustainable community may have contributed to this confusion. A workable definition which focuses on the need to make communities work for everyone could facilitate a constructive discussion about meeting the twin objectives of sustainable communities and rehousing for those in urgent need.

Where there are housing shortages, and shortages of investment for new homes, people in housing need will inevitably be concentrated in deprived areas as they wait for a better offer of housing. Tackling this will require an increase in affordable housing options in areas of high housing stress.

About the research

The research focused on the implications of new approaches to lettings. Although limited to England, the study has examined the experiences of both local authorities and registered social landlords.

The objectives of the research have been to:

- examine the range of approaches to letting social housing

- assess the impact of these on the rehousing prospects of those in urgent housing need, including homeless households

- assist Shelter in identifying good practice in lettings which can resolve tensions between meeting individual housing need and addressing other housing or community objectives.

One of the key research findings has been the poor level and quality of monitoring and evaluation by landlords implementing new lettings policies. For this reason it has been extremely difficult to gauge with accuracy the impact of such policies on households in need.

The research was carried out in four stages:

- interviews with relevant national organisations to gather background information and build on a review of recent and current research

- a telephone survey of a stratified random sample of 65 social landlords (local authorities and RSLs) to find out about new approaches to lettings

- a telephone survey of a sample of 40 social landlords (local authorities and RSLs) chosen because they have adopted new approaches to lettings

- interviews and analysis of data in five case study organisations (CDS Housing, London Borough of Lewisham, Notting Hill Housing Trust, Rochdale Metropolitan Borough Council and Sheffield City Council).

Key findings

The research has confirmed both the complexity of the lettings process and the many different objectives which it can be expected to meet. There are often clear tensions between these different objectives. For example, meeting the requirements of those in priority housing need may not be seen as compatible with making lettings which address community needs in a wider sense.

There are problems with the current system. One example is the use of multiple criteria for measuring different aspects of need may result in overly complex systems of needs assessment, and policies and practices which are not always easily understood. But the evidence suggests that most social landlords are still seeking to prioritise lettings according to needs-based criteria.

The way lettings are organised varies considerably between social landlords. Our first-stage random sample of social landlords suggested a preponderance of centralised letting functions, but this was not mirrored either by the second stage study of innovative practice or by the case studies, where decentralised systems were the norm.

Where organisations have made changes to their allocation policy, three underlying themes with clear resonance for the Government have emerged:

- restricting access through the use of exclusions

- opening up access to 'non-traditional' groups

- creating and maintaining more sustainable communities.

Many landlords have incorporated a variety of approaches within a single policy. Over half of the random sample of social landlords had made changes to the criteria for assessing housing need, in many cases to reflect the change of emphasis given in the Housing Act 1996 to the rehousing of homeless and vulnerable households. Almost half had either made changes to their policies on exclusions, or introduced such a policy for the first time. Almost 20 per cent of landlords had changed the extent to which they use local lettings policies. A significant number said they planned reviews to one or more elements of their lettings policies.

From an analysis of both the random and innovation surveys, it was possible to identify a number of new approaches to lettings which involved one or more of the following:

- changes (increases and decreases) in the extent to which exclusions and/or suspensions of applicants were used
- widening the range of applicants from which lettings could be made
- speeding up the process and reducing bureaucracy
- changes in the degree of scrutiny applied to applications
- applying different criteria to the assessment and prioritisation of applicants with the aim of getting a different mix of tenants
- relaxing eligibility rules so that households can under-occupy properties
- the amount of officer discretion in decisions about lettings.

Motivation for change varied between local authorities and RSLs. While local authorities were primarily motivated by the Housing Act 1996 changes, RSLs have responded to a combination of internal organisational changes and external pressures including crime and disorder. Four broad themes emerged:

- changing demand
- the competing interests of new and existing tenants
- the experience of communities when certain types of household have been rehoused
- wider debates about sustainable communities and the role of social housing.

Local authorities and RSLs have applied a wide variety of exclusions and suspensions, either from the housing register or from consideration for rehousing, although relatively few of them indicated that they had changed their policy on exclusions since the 1996 Act. RSLs more commonly excluded applicants than local authorities. In our random sample, 51 out of 65 organisations surveyed operated suspension policies.

The most common reported reasons for exclusions were debt from current or former social housing tenancies and past anti-social behaviour. Most debt exclusions were for housing debt, but a few landlords excluded on the basis of other debt, notably council tax. Debt was also the basis for most suspensions from the waiting list. In the majority of cases debts had to be cleared before an applicant was accepted or re-instated on the housing register.

Where social landlords excluded on the basis of anti-social behaviour there was a wide difference in the type of behaviour considered anti-social and the level of proof required. A minority required a legal stage in possession proceedings to have been reached as a basis for exclusion. Most left the decision open to interpretation.

It is of continuing concern that, despite advice to the contrary, local authorities and RSLs which exclude applicants from their housing registers do not rountinely monitor their exclusions. Only a third of organisations surveyed undertook any monitoring of either the number of or the reasons for exclusion.

It is clear that there are major differences of approach to exclusion, for example on whether to exclude outright or apply a penalty. Lack of monitoring makes it impossible to say how exclusions affect particular groups, especially homeless applicants.

Over half of the organisations reporting new approaches to lettings indicated trying to widen the range of potential applicants. In the random sample the proportion was over a third.

A desire to create or maintain sustainable communities was a major factor in a wide range of local policy changes. Most organisations were trying to achieve this aim by applying different criteria to the assessment and prioritisation of applicants. Many organisations were unclear about exactly what constituted a sustainable community.

Local lettings policies are one approach to creating sustainable communities. They have been adopted by almost 30 per cent of the landlords in the random survey for three broad reasons:

- **tackling unpopular estates**

- **achieving 'balanced' communities**

- **maintaining the stability of established areas.**

These policies were often one part of a package of measures aimed at tackling a particular problem. Most of the policies involved seeking to attract new types of applicants, the tighter use of selection criteria and a wider use of exclusions.

Most of the social landlords which had introduced local lettings policies believed they were meeting their objectives. However, several noted that this had often been a subjective assessment. In many instances the degree of monitoring and evaluation of such schemes has been limited, which makes it difficult to assess their strengths and weaknesses. It must be recognised that social landlords have limited scope to manipulate the social balance of a particular estate or area through the lettings process. It may be that developing mixed tenure schemes, rather than just changing lettings policies, may be a more appropriate response.

Evidence of wide variation and inconsistency in the application of lettings policies both within and between social landlords emerged when they were asked to say what approach they would adopt in 12 anonymous cases. This included the use of exclusions and the degree of choice offered to different applicants.

There is a need for more effective monitoring and evaluation of lettings policies from the point of application, where exclusions and suspensions may be applied, to the actual housing situations of successful (and unsuccessful) applicants.

Policy implications and key recommendations

Whatever system is in place, social housing lettings policies need to be transparent.

Applicants need to know:

- whether they are eligible for housing (in which areas, and of what type and size)
- how to apply and understand the system
- how priority is awarded
- how to appeal if they are not satisfied with the way their application is handled
- what information they should expect to receive, and when.

Lettings policies should continue to emphasise needs-based criteria, although there is certainly potential for a simpler system for assessing housing need.

Wider choice for both new and existing tenants should be promoted, although the degree of choice which can be offered will vary according to local housing market conditions.

There is also a need to move towards greater equity of choice between the different access routes to social housing. If equity is not attainable, perhaps there is scope for an approach which guarantees that all offers will meet certain criteria, such as being in one of an applicant's stated areas of preference.

The research has shown wide variation in the use of exclusions by social landlords. While there may be a case for exclusion in certain circumstances, the use of 'blanket' exclusions from the register of particular groups is not appropriate. This was recognised by the Government in the Homes Bill. However, there is also a need for closer monitoring of the use of exclusions and suspensions and clear guidance to applicants as to how these can be removed.

Monitoring of lettings needs to be improved to prevent unfairness and unwanted outcomes. This can also help in developing policy responses to problems of mismatch between housing supply and demand.

There is a strong argument in favour of a greater emphasis on a strategic approach to lettings which recognises the potential for using transfers. Transfers can satisfy the requirements and preferences of existing tenants needing or wishing to move and at the same time create vacancies which can be used to help general applicants in priority need.

While there may be scope for further guidance on who should be able to gain access to social rented housing and how applicants should be prioritised, there remains a need for continued flexibility and autonomy at a local level.

Lettings policies (and local policies in respect of specific areas, estates, or blocks of property) need to be based on an effective local analysis of housing market conditions. This analysis needs to assess the likely supply of and demand for social housing from different groups as well as reflecting broader national policies and directives.

This will enable the impact of local schemes on a wider area to be quantified. If this is not done, the danger is that people in need may be squeezed out of a number of localised schemes. Proper analysis is important in the context of neighbourhood renewal. Assessment of the impact of localised lettings policies on a wider area should be taken by local authorities as part of the development of homelessness prevention strategies and shared with all local landlords and local strategic partnerships.

Chapter 1:

Introduction

1.1 Background

The principle that social rented housing should be allocated to those households in the greatest housing need has long been widely accepted (CHAC, 1949; CHAC, 1969; DoE, 1978). That does not always mean that the principle has been turned into practice. Less than a decade ago the Institute of Housing published research showing that, although only a small minority of local authorities were clinging to what were described as the 'worst type of policies' (IoH,1990, p74), access was by no means open. And there was little correlation between market demands, the supply of rehousing opportunities and the restrictiveness of letting policies.

A succession of studies has demonstrated the efficiency of local authorities and registered social landlords (RSLs) in developing and implementing access and letting systems and policies which both address needs and minimise vacancies and rent loss (Bines et al, 1993; Griffiths et al, 1997; Parker et al, 1992). However, some social landlords believe that needs-based mechanisms are not working in some areas. The suggestion is that as a result of this social landlords are increasingly using criteria other than just housing need in their letting policies.

It is recognised that lettings policies are underpinned by a number of objectives, some of which may be in conflict. For example, giving applicants priority according to housing need may not always appear to fit in with landlords' desire to promote more sustainable, mixed communities.

While central Government may issue guidance on the operation of lettings (DETR, 1999a), local authorities and registered social landlords, within an overall framework, have considerable freedom to devise their own letting systems reflecting local circumstances.

This diversity has been reflected in a number of ways, but falls into two main categories:

- **widening access** to social housing through the use of 'local lettings' policies or other policies which reflect criteria other than just housing need
- **narrowing access** to social housing through policies which exclude certain individuals, households or groups of people, either because of ineligibility or previous unacceptable behaviour, real or perceived.

This study took place before the significant policy shifts articulated in the Housing Green Paper (DETR/DSS, 2000a), 'The way forward for housing' (DETR/DSS, 2000c) and the Homes Bill, which set out a new agenda for access to social housing. The changing framework underpinning neighbourhood renewal schemes, with the advent of the National Strategy for Neighbourhood Renewal and the Neighbourhood Renewal Unit, is also significant. These take as their starting point the policy action team (PAT) reports to the Social Exclusion Unit. The PAT report on housing management (DETR, 1999b) emphasised that letting policies are significant in shaping the profile of an estate, the demands on the housing management service and the sustainability of communities. It recognised that many social landlords have been developing lettings plans which seek to take account of the needs of areas as a whole, as well as those of the individual.

Everyone accepts that in areas of severe housing pressure there is less scope for policies which depart from criteria which are more strictly based on housing need. However, it has also been argued that experience in the UK and elsewhere suggests that letting policies should aim to promote the stability of particular neighbourhoods by taking other factors into account.

Nationally, the evidence is of significant unmet need for affordable housing (Kleinman et al, 1999). Although the level of local authority homeless acceptances has been falling since 1991, it was still nearly twice as high in 1999 as it was in 1980, while the number of homeless households in temporary accommodation exceeded 62,000 in 1999. Households in bed and breakfast and hostels in 1999 were three times as great as the number in 1980 (Wilcox, 1999). There is also evidence of expanding housing registers and problems of accessing and/or sustaining housing in other tenures. This must be seen in the context of wider social changes; historically high levels of unemployment, relationship breakdown, a policy shift to independent living (as opposed to institutional life), increasing social polarisation and exclusion, and changing relationships between incomes and housing costs.

In many areas there remains a shortage of permanent affordable good quality housing available for letting, either via vacancies or through nominations to RSLs. The loss of council stock, primarily under the right to buy, has not been fully off-set by new housing provision through RSLs, and although they are now expected to make a greater contribution than in the past to addressing local housing needs, their output of new completions is only about the same as it was in 1980.

Whilst the current rate of provision of affordable housing nationally is significantly below that which is necessary to meet housing need, recent research has pointed to evidence of changing demand for social rented housing in some parts of the country, reflected in relatively high turnover of tenancies, high vacancy rates and increasing difficulties experienced in letting properties (Cole et al, 1999; Holmans and Simpson,

1999; Murie et al, 1998). There are many factors behind this changing demand, and many are beyond the control of housing policy and practice alone. Changes in supply, both in the social sector and other tenures, and in the quality of supply, also impact upon housing choice, and therefore demand. The precise relationship between these two processes will vary according to location, and whilst the scale of low demand for social housing may be greater in the North of England it is also apparent in parts of the South. There are significant implications for UK housing policy as a result of changing patterns of housing need and the demand for social housing.

Some commentators have argued that restrictive letting policies have helped to create problems within communities by preventing more affluent households from gaining access to social housing (Young and Lemos, 1997). Many social landlords have relaxed their allocation policies, at least in relation to parts of their stock. However, in doing so they may have increased turnover, and introduced a new kind of instability, by encouraging access for young households and single people, many of whom may regard social housing as a temporary solution to their housing needs.

It is necessary to understand the processes which are driving changing demand for social housing, and to consider these at a local level. Local responses to real or perceived problems may involve changes to the approaches taken by social landlords to lettings. At the same time, there is a need to assess how the implementation of such policies at a local level impacts upon different households and the extent to which they are effective in meeting their objectives.

There are significant implications for housing management in general, and for lettings in particular, as a result of the changing context within which social rented housing operates. But it is important to recognise that changes in the wider policy context of health, crime, education, employment and other key services are essential if the problems evident in social housing are to be tackled effectively.

1.2   Objectives

The research focused on the implications of new approaches to lettings. Although limited to England the study examined the experiences of both local authorities and registered social landlords.

The objectives of the research were to:

- examine the range of approaches to the allocation of social housing

- assess the impact of these on the rehousing prospects of those in urgent housing need, including homeless households

- assist Shelter in identifying good practice in allocations which can resolve tensions between meeting individual housing need and addressing other housing or community objectives.

- One of the key research findings has been the poor level and quality of monitoring and evaluation by landlords implementing new lettings policies. For this reason it has been extremely difficult to gauge with accuracy the impact of such policies on households in need.

1.3 Research methods

The research was undertaken in four stages between Summer 1999 and Spring 2000.

1. Background/national context

As part of the context setting for the research, and building upon a review of current and recent research on lettings, interviews were conducted with a range of relevant national organisations: Department of the Environment, Transport and the Regions (DETR), Housing Corporation, Local Government Association, National Housing Federation, National Homeless Alliance, Northern Consortium of Housing Authorities, and Tenants and Residents Organisation of England.

2. Stage one telephone survey: the national picture

To develop a representative national picture for England of the different approaches to lettings, the use of local lettings policies and the extent of exclusions, a stratified random sample of 52 local authorities and 30 RSLs was used for a stage one telephone interview survey. This is referred to as the 'random survey'. The methodology is set out in more detail in Appendix 1.

3. Stage two telephone survey: innovative approaches to lettings

A second stage telephone survey was conducted with 28 additional social landlords. This represented a mix of type and size of organisation and different types of local policy, underpinned by different rationales. The stage two respondents were identified either through stage one contact, via the Chartered Institute of Housing's Good Practice Unit (GPU) or from the housing press. This 'innovation survey' is explained in more detail in Appendix 1.

4. Case Studies

Five organisations were selected for more detailed investigation (see Appendix 1 for more details):

- **CDS Housing.** An RSL with 4,825 homes which operates in the North West of England, with its highest concentrations of properties in Liverpool and Halton in Cheshire. The organisation is experiencing relatively low demand for some of its stock, the inability of local authorities to provide nominations to vacancies, and relatively high turnover of tenancies. Whilst its lettings policy prioritises housing need, it is developing more flexible policies where the supply of vacancies exceeds demand.

- **London Borough of Lewisham.** An inner London authority with 32,000 homes. There are enormous rehousing pressures within the borough, and the council gives priority to households with no permanent or secure housing, families, households containing vulnerable people and existing tenants with urgent transfer needs, or where rehousing would release much-needed accommodation elsewhere. As part of an overall lettings strategy there are also policies to encourage transfers where this will help to make more effective use of the housing stock.

- **Notting Hill Housing Trust.** This RSL has 12,900 homes in West London in an area of relatively high housing need, with high levels of demand for accommodation in the social rented sector. The main aim of the Trust is to provide rented housing for those on low incomes or occupying inadequate housing, but at the same time it has sought to address social polarisation on its estates, through the active promotion of mixed communities.

- **Rochdale Metropolitan Borough Council.** Total stock of 17,000 homes. In many parts of the borough there is an over-supply of social housing and difficulties in letting (not restricted to the local authority). Rochdale is in economic decline, with a drift of population to more prosperous areas of Greater Manchester, and council housing's image has declined, such that it has become the 'tenure of last resort'. To help overcome these fundamental problems the Council has introduced a fast-track rehousing service, 'Selectahome'. This is considered in more detail in Chapter 2.

- **Sheffield Metropolitan Borough Council.** Facing low demand for many of its properties (18,500 out of 65,000 are judged to be difficult to let). There is evidence of an over-supply of social rented housing and evidence of increasing polarisation within the city, with the west and south thriving while the north and east are in decline. A wide range of initiatives have been put in place in response to changes in demand, including a help desk whose staff facilitate a fast-track route into local authority accommodation. Research undertaken by the council has shown that a significant reduction in the size of the social rented sector is needed if the problem of falling demand is not to become even more acute.

The case study approach

In each case study organisation we have sought to use four different, yet complementary, approaches to assess the impact of different allocation policies at a local level. These were:

- face-to-face (and, where appropriate, supplementary telephone) interviews with key officers within each of the case study organisations, as well as some of the main agencies providing or accepting nominations/referrals. These interviews examined barriers to access, rehousing priorities, policies on transfers, exchanges, nominations and referrals, arrangements for rehousing homeless applicants, policies on offers and refusals, issues of choice and equity, and the monitoring of allocations decisions and outcomes.

- the use of the organisation's own monitoring data on applications, lettings, refusals etc.

- the collection of data on a small cohort of applicants re-housed in the case study area, focusing on outcomes both before and after the change in the letting system which followed the Housing Act 1996. However, this information was only collected in three of the case studies, and it has proved extremely difficult at a local level to assess the impact of changes in letting policies and procedures as to whether some households have received enhanced priority while others may have had to wait longer for permanent housing. It is extremely difficult to look at specific estates or areas in isolation from wider housing markets and other factors which may have shaped either landlords' decisions or applicants' choice. More detailed district-wide longitudinal analysis may be appropriate in the future.

- the use of a small number of anonymous real applications for rehousing in order to test these against local allocation policies with both policy officers and front-line housing staff.

1.4 The changing context

The local authority housing stock declined from just over 5 million homes in 1981 to just over 3.3 million in 1998; a fall of just over a third. Table 1.1 shows that this decline has continued over the last two years. Over a similar period the RSL sector in England has grown from 422,000 homes in 1981 to more than a million in 1998. Whilst new local authority housing completions have declined from over 67,000 homes in 1980 to just 251 in 1998, between 1986 and 1998 new completions by RSLs averaged over 19,000 a year, and were slightly higher in 1998 than they had been in 1980.

However, as was noted in the opening section, recent policy debates have been dominated by evidence of an increased need for affordable housing nationally (Kleinman et al, 1999) alongside changing demand for housing in particular localities (especially parts of the North of England). The emerging agenda has been about how to respond to changing demand (Cole et al, 1999; Holmans and Simpson, 1999; Murie et al, 1998). Analysis by Pawson (1998) has identified that, despite the decline in the local authority stock, the annual number of lettings to new tenants has remained relatively constant. Lettings to new tenants in England by local authorities declined from 255,000 in 1982/83 to 228,000 in 1989/90, but increased to 260,000 in 1996/97 (Wilcox, 1999, p203). However, there are regional differences in the pattern of local authority lettings to new tenants. The Northern and Midland regions saw a rapid increase in the 1990s, while in London (particularly) and the South East the number of lettings to new tenants has declined since 1991/92.

A number of reasons have been put forward to explain this rise in turnover. These include the changing profile of tenants in the sector (the over representation of older and younger households, and the 'hollowing out' of the middle aged group), shifts in attitudes and preferences, the poor image of social rented housing (with media references to the links between social housing and crime, deprivation, poverty and social exclusion), and a general exodus into the private sector.

The pattern of lettings in the RSL sector is slightly different, as a result of continuing new provision during the 1980s and 1990s, with a greater proportion of tenants in the younger age groups. However, again there is evidence of increasing turnover in parts of this sector.

Of course, increased turnover is not necessarily associated with low demand. The evidence from local authority housing registers is that there are still considerable numbers of people on waiting lists for council housing. The figures for 1999 (Table 1.1) show more than a million applicants on local authority housing registers. This represents a demand for a third of the total local authority stock, with generally higher levels of demand in Yorkshire and Humberside, the South East, the South West and East Midlands. Local authorities report that more than 80 per cent of those on the housing register are in housing need.

TABLE 1.1   Local authority dwellings, difficult-to-let (DTL) stock and numbers on housing registers, by region, England 1999

Region	Dwelling Stock	DTL Stock	%	Housing register (exc. transfers)	%	Housing register in need	%
North East	286,353	47,310	17	66,028	23	53,147	19
Yorkshire/ Humberside	426,990	63,888	15	172,221	40	113,548	27
East Midlands	279,159	28,904	10	100,575	36	70,164	25
East	289,384	15,786	5	91,948	32	75,304	26
London	569,214	40,199	7	196,335	35	184,516	32
South East	262,175	8,827	3	111,341	42	97,499	37
South West	184,152	3,496	2	84,983	46	73,558	40
West Midlands	381,034	41,591	11	95,857	25	81,932	22
North West	471,727	79,495	17	119,436	25	93,174	20
ENGLAND	3,150,188	329,496	10	1,038,724	33	842,842	27

Source: DETR housing investment programme data

TABLE 1.2   Local authority and registered social landlord lettings by region, England 1998/99

Region	Lettings to new secure tenants	Priority homeless No.	%	Lettings to new non-secure tenants	Priority homeless No.	%	RSL lettings (inc. nominations, exc. transfers)	Priority homeless No.	%
London	19,897	9,781	49	12,063	7,146	59	15,843	4,038	25
South East	12,382	3,180	26	4,604	3,707	81	20,403	4,013	20
South West	8,624	2,086	24	4,282	1,970	46	10,995	2,031	18
East	14,905	3,381	23	3,386	2,707	80	13,682	1,859	14
East Midlands	19,951	2,814	14	6,004	1,737	29	9,636	1,188	12
West Midlands	24,056	6,335	26	7,856	1,265	16	14,264	1,308	9
Yorkshire/ Humberside	32,618	5,267	16	5,248	1,513	29	13,391	650	5
North East	3,811	495	13	21,309	2,597	12	7,280	266	4
North West	25,398	2,460	10	22,830	2,713	12	22,634	822	4
ENGLAND	161,622	35,799	22	87,582	25,255	29	128,128	16,175	13

Source: DETR housing investment programme data

Housing registers are imperfect indicators of the demand for social housing. Local eligibility criteria vary considerably and there is widespread use of exclusions. The number of people registering may also be influenced by perceptions of the supply of suitable housing by applicants. At the same time housing registers are not static. Applicants' circumstances change and review processes may take time to catch up. In addition, registers may include applications which are, either by choice or as a result of decisions by the landlord, 'deferred', 'suspended' or 'inactive'. It may be more appropriate to consider the relationship, not between numbers on the housing register and the stock of housing, but between the flows of vacancies (supply) on the one hand and new applications, deletions, lettings and nominations (effective demand) on the other. The housing register figures hide not only weaknesses in data but also wide variations in expressed preference for social housing at a very local level.

While social landlords may be reporting considerable demand for social housing, in many cases there will be wide variations between considerable demand for certain properties in particular areas and much less demand for other properties in different areas. Local authorities have more than one million applicants on their housing registers, but they are also reporting between nine and ten per cent of their housing stock is difficult to let. Again, there are variations in the proportions of the stock classified in this way, with higher proportions in the northern regions and the West Midlands (and much lower in the East, South East and South West regions). However, these regional figures also hide much wider variations.

More than 20 years ago it was accepted that the factors which lead to social housing becoming difficult to let have serious implications for the housing service as a whole, and that changes to lettings are one measure in a possible package of measures (DoE, 1980). More recently it was noted that 61 per cent of English local authorities reported areas of low demand or unpopular housing, accounting for 11.5 per cent of the stock (DETR, 1999d). Earlier research has suggested at least 4 per cent of RSL stock was considered difficult to let (Pawson et al, 1997), and this at a time when the proportion of local authority difficult-to-let stock was reported as only six per cent. Again, the evidence is of wide regional and local variation.

Table 1.2 shows the number and proportion of new local authority and RSL lettings in 1998/99 made to priority homeless households, as a further indicator of housing need. The evidence from the 1980s and early 1990s is of a growth in the number of homeless acceptances in England, from just under 63,000 in 1980 rising to almost 94,000 in 1985 and nearly 152,000 in 1991. The comparable figure has fallen to just under 112,000 in 1999 (DETR, 2000b). This has led to increased pressures on temporary accommodation and to an increase in the proportion of new lettings being made to homeless households. This proportion increased from 19 per cent in 1982/83 to 46 per cent in 1991/92, although this has since declined to 25 per cent in 1997/98 (Wilcox, 1999, p203).

Table 1.2 also illustrates the regional differences in the proportions of both new secure and non-secure lettings which have been made to priority homeless households in 1998/99. The majority of new lettings made have been secure tenancies, although a significant (and growing) proportion have been on a non-secure basis. Overall, just over a fifth of all new secure lettings have been to priority homeless households, although this hides significant regional differences, with more than twice this proportion of secure lettings in London being to homeless people, while the proportion allocated to homeless people in the North East, North West and East Midlands have been well below the national average. Outside London, the trend has been for a significant fall in the proportion of new secure lettings going to homeless households since 1992/93.

The figures in Table 1.2 also show that a higher proportion of new non-secure lettings have been made to priority homeless households, although the proportion does appear to be declining, no doubt reflecting the practice adopted by some individual authorities of using introductory tenancies. Once more, there are wide regional variations in the proportion of these lettings made to priority homeless people, which generally have been higher in the South of England and much lower in the North.

The evidence from housing investment programme (HIP) returns indicates that 13 per cent of RSL lettings in 1998/99 were to priority homeless households, with higher proportions in London and the rest of the South East and much lower proportions in the North East and North West regions. Information from RSL lettings data for 1998/99 (Universities of St Andrews and Dundee, 2000) suggests that just under 20 per cent of all general needs lettings were to homeless households (statutory and non-statutory), though this figure has fallen from a third in 1993/94. This data also shows that the proportion of general needs lettings by RSLs to statutory homeless people has declined since 1993/94.

So far this section has sought to establish how the context for social housing lettings has changed. In particular, demographic and continued household growth have led to concerns about a mismatch between housing supply and housing need and demand. At the same time, there has been widespread debate about low and changing demand for housing in parts of the country, together with the unpopularity of particular types of housing or housing in particular places, even in areas of overall relatively high demand for social housing.

Despite the decline in the scale of local authority housing in the 1980s and 1990s, the level of new lettings has been more or less been sustained because turnover in the sector has increased. There is evidence of considerable demand for social rented housing, with more than one million households currently on local authority housing registers. Whilst the registers have limitations, they do reflect demand being expressed for social housing and, following the 1996 Act, have been given a firmer statutory foundation. However, registers need to be analysed in terms of how they are changing and of the local context in which they operate, as well as at a disaggregated level, in terms of expressed demand for housing at a local area or estate level.

The issue of changing demand for social housing is affecting every landlord and every locality to a greater or lesser degree. However, precisely what is happening, in terms of changes in demand, shifts in supply and the exercise of choice is subject to considerable variation, depending upon the precise interaction of a range of factors. As a result policy responses also need to vary at a local level, and in particular policies on access to and the allocation of social housing need to be seen in the context of a range of policy responses.

1.5 The background to changing lettings policies

The Housing Act 1996 represented a major review and amendment of the law in relation to homelessness, housing advice and the allocation of social housing in England and Wales.

Parts VI and VII were seen as having seven main objectives:

- to bring together the two main routes into council housing, waiting lists and homelessness, and combine them into a single access route which also covers nominations to registered social landlords

- to create a framework that would allow central Government to dictate how councils should let housing, leaving discretion to social landlords locally to determine how policies are developed and implemented

- to assess the needs of homeless and non-homeless applicants in the same way, attempting to differentiate between those with short-term and long-term housing need

- to restrict access for asylum seekers and other groups of people from abroad

- to extend the use of the private rented sector for homeless households

- to clarify the law in the wake of the Awua judgement

- to place a new emphasis on the role of housing advice in alleviating housing stress (Chartered Institute of Housing, 1996).

Prior to the passage of the legislation there was widespread opposition to the proposals, and particularly to the view that it was necessary to curtail the rights of homeless people in order to secure a fairer system of letting social housing. The incoming 1997 Labour Government added certain categories of homeless households to those to whom local authorities must give 'reasonable preference' in their letting schemes. At the same time, more emphasis was given to strategic approaches to homelessness, more broadly defined than just those to whom local authorities have a duty, to meet wider needs. An important element of such strategies has been the provision of advice, information, support and outreach services.

Most local authorities have locally determined policies which, within the legislative framework, prescribe admission to the housing register and the ways in which rehousing priority is governed. Most RSLs also usually maintain their own housing registers (though in some places common housing registers have been established), to which local authorities have nominations rights, often for 50 per cent or more of true vacancies.

Social housing lettings have usually been underpinned by the principal objective of meeting the most urgent housing needs. However, systems have often allowed a degree of flexibility to allow social landlords to develop overall rehousing strategies which respond to a range of needs, as well as offering some prospects of meeting applicants' housing preferences. In the last few years it has been argued (Page, 1993; DETR, 1999d) that letting policies should should help to create sustainable local communities as well as meet the needs of individual households. The concern here is that letting policies may exacerbate the problems in particular areas by increasing the concentrations of disadvantaged and socially excluded people.

Critics of existing social housing letting systems point to the fact that they can often be overly complicated in their attempts to measure need. As a result, they can be difficult to explain to consumers and difficult to understand for officers and councillors. Systems are often seen as bureaucratic and lacking in transparency. It has also been argued that letting policies have offered little choice, even in areas of relatively low demand, sometimes penalising applicants who refuse reasonable offers of housing. Those who accept social housing on the basis of 'Hobson's Choice' may start out with negative views of the tenure. At the same time, differences in the use of eligibility criteria by social landlords and the exclusion of groups of people from consideration for rehousing may be unfair and add to the problems of social exclusion. Alternatively, a lack of sensitivity in lettings may create problems not only for housing managers but also for existing residents.

The current Government sees the allocation of social housing as an essential tool in its overall housing strategy. Its Housing Green Paper set out proposals to encourage the reform of lettings to give those seeking social housing greater choice over their homes (DETR/DSS, 2000a).

Future primary legislation is likely to address issues of access and lettings in England and Wales. In the meantime it is important to consider what changes have been taking place in the policies and practices of local authorities and RSLs, and what impact these may have had.

1.6 About the report

Chapter 2 examines the organisation of the allocations process. It begins by asking what social housing lettings are trying to achieve and how systems are organised in different social landlord organisations. It examines the extent to which letting policies have changed in the light of the Housing Act 1996, what have been the motivations for change, and how those changes have been implemented. In particular it examines the issue of exclusions from rehousing (restricting access), the opening up of access to a wider range of applicants, and moves towards more sustainable communities.

Chapter 3 focuses on the extent to which social landlords have developed local or community lettings policies for parts of their stock, where this has been done and why. Local variations in lettings policies are examined as responses to particular local problems and issues. The chapter also considers the strategic use of transfers in certain areas to make better use of the stock and to address a range of housing needs.

Chapter 4 considers the impact of different letting policies and looks at the outcomes of different approaches in terms of who gets housed. It also examines issues raised by monitoring of the lettings process.

Finally, in Chapter 5 we draw together the different aspects of the study and highlight the tensions between making individual lettings which meet priority housing need (and which offer applicants a degree of choice and do not unduly exclude from consideration those with urgent rehousing need) and lettings policies which, taken as a whole, help to create sustainable and harmonious communities. This chapter concludes that letting policies (and local letting policies) need to be based upon an effective local analysis of housing market conditions, as well as reflecting broader national policies and directives.

Chapter 2:

Lettings: recent changes in policy and practice

2.1 Introduction: messages from Government and social housing regulators

Changing messages about what lettings policy and practice should be aiming to achieve have emerged from the Government over the past year. The consistent themes are: building viable and sustainable communities; avoiding concentrations of people with certain attributes; and promoting choice for housing applicants. The relative weight of these factors in developing local policies has not been addressed.

The Department of the Environment, Transport and the Regions (DETR) draft Code of Guidance for local authorities on allocation of accommodation and homelessness urges local authorities to ensure that letting policies do not lead to vulnerable or homeless people being rehoused in the less popular areas of a district (DETR, 1999a, paragraph 5.30). It states that authorities should have the same regard for the preferences of homeless applicants as for the preferences of other applicants, even if homeless applicants are made one offer while other applicants are made more than one offer. It also notes that flexibility within letting schemes may be used by authorities to select tenants for property on a new estate in a way which ensures a range of social and economic groups (paragraph 5.17).

Housing investment programme guidance provided to local authorities in 1999 reinforced the message on sustainable communities, but also emphasised the importance of meeting the needs of homeless households (DETR, 1999c).

In December 1999, the Housing Corporation issued an addendum to its social housing standards for general and supported housing outlining an approach to tackling anti-social behaviour which encompassed lettings, housing management and residents' rights. Specifically, the guidance stated: 'RSLs should take action at the lettings stage to ensure that they do not create concentrations of people who may either have difficulty in sustaining their tenancy, or have a history of anti-social behaviour' (Housing Corporation, 1999, p2).

Reports from the Social Exclusion Unit's policy action teams on housing management (PAT 5) and unpopular housing (PAT 7) both contained recommendations on lettings. PAT 5 concluded that 'letting policies that are sensitive to the community and to the need to relieve social exclusion are desirable for the long term stability of an area'(DETR, 1999b). PAT 7 recommended that the DETR should promote pilots in local authorities experiencing low demand to release a proportion of new lettings through an advertising scheme. It suggested that DETR should discuss ways in which the 'local connection' requirements for access to social rented housing could be relaxed to ensure the best use of all the housing stock in London and other large cities where there is a high demand for social housing. The report emphasised the importance of moving housing organisations towards a more market-oriented culture, including the provision of training for staff with emphasis on a customer focused approach to service provision (DETR, 1999d).

The introduction of best value and tenant participation compacts also has implications for allocations policies and practices. A new duty on local authorities to promote the social, economic and environmental well-being of the community may result in the need for a more corporate approach to determining the policy priorities for lettings (LGA, 1999). In addition, consultation with tenants and other service users on priorities, resources and service standards will require a more transparent approach to developing and reviewing policy.

The Homes Bill set out a new agenda for lettings which attempted to implement policies set out in the Housing Green Paper (DETR/DSS, 2000a) and 'The way forward for housing' (DETR/DSS, 2000c) to end blanket exclusions and replace these with suspensions. The Homes Bill also set out a duty on local authorities to develop strategies to prevent homelessness. Lettings policies would play a central role in achieving this.

Given this context from the Government and regulators of social housing, as well as the legislative context provided by the Housing Act 1996, what approaches are local authorities and registered social landlords taking to the letting of their housing stock?

2.2 What is the lettings process trying to achieve?

Previous research has set out a number of policy objectives which can underpin a lettings policy. In practice, some of these objectives will conflict with each other. In particular, it may be difficult to reconcile developing communities which avoid social polarisation with giving applicants priority according to housing need. This tension is one which is at the centre of current debates about the future direction of letting policies. It is also reflected in the aims and objectives of the lettings policies of organisations participating in this research.

The objectives of lettings set out by the five case study organisations differ significantly in the extent to which this tension is reflected. The lettings of allocations at CDS Housing are most clearly focused on meeting housing need, letting properties, maximising rental income, reducing voids and void times.

In contrast Notting Hill Housing Trust sets out a broader set of objectives for its allocation policy which:

- looks at the wider context of individuals' housing needs as well as their shelter

- acknowledges the relationship between the housing market and local economies and communities

- supports local labour force needs of local communities

- actively plans for mixed communities to decrease social polarisation

- sets housing policies within the context of social policies.

2.3 How are access and lettings organised?

The activities associated with the lettings function are set out below, although local practice varies:

- receiving applications from various access routes

- assessing and prioritising them

- maintaining a housing register or waiting list

- matching applicants with vacancies

- making offers

- producing information about rehousing opportunities

- developing and reviewing policy and procedures

- reviewing the service

- monitoring the outcomes of lettings

- communicating with applicants at all stages of the process, including the provision of advice.

Of the 65 local authorities and RSLs responding to the random survey, just under a third (18) stated that they had a decentralised allocations function, while over two thirds (46) had a centralised function. Well over a third (25) of the 65 organisations participated in one or more common housing registers. Of these, seven had a common lettings policy and 12 had adopted a common approach to exclusions from the register.

The predominance of a centralised lettings function indicated by the results of the
random survey was not mirrored by responses to the innovation survey (or by the
arrangements in place within case study organisations which are summarised
below). Over half the organisations which responded to the innovation survey had a
decentralised lettings function.

CDS Housing maintains a waiting list centrally. Assessment of applications
for rehousing are also carried out centrally, while lettings are carried out at
three area offices. CDS operates a system of multiple waiting lists, with a list
for each property type within each lettings area organised on the basis of post
codes. Each waiting list has a points threshold below which applicants will not
be accepted. The aim of the organisation is that no applicant should be on a
waiting list for more than six months before being rehoused.

The London Borough of Lewisham has a decentralised lettings policy operated
from 16 neighbourhood offices. The policy had been operating for just over a
year at the time of the case study and applicants were organised through a
single register (general applicants, homeless households and transfer
applicants) with priority categories for rehousing and then a points system
within the priority categories. Applications are usually made to the local
neighbourhood office, whilst homeless households normally applied through
the council's homeless persons unit. Specific quotas are set aside for those with
social care and health needs, and with voluntary agencies for 'move on'
accommodation, although these are small numbers. There is a centralised team
which provides policy support and service development to the neighbourhoods,
as well as monitoring the process.

Notting Hill Housing Trust has a specialist and decentralised lettings function.
Each of the three areas of the organisation is responsible for devising its own
lettings plan relating primarily to new developments, but this also involves
setting targets for particular groups, for example, those under-represented in
local communities such as certain minority ethnic groups. The trust does not
maintain its own waiting list, electing instead to allocate all its vacancies via
nominations, referrals and transfers. The percentage of local authority
nominations varies between areas and schemes, but can be up to 100 per cent.

In Rochdale MBC, mainstream lettings are carried out by five area offices,
while Selectahome (fast-track) lettings, nominations and out-of-town lettings
(mobility) are carried out centrally. The central rehousing team is also
responsible for the development of policies and procedures relating to
allocations, advising area offices on these policies and procedures, and
supervising and monitoring the lettings function. The housing register, which
includes transfer applicants, is not organised into specific categories but it is
possible to select applicants by a wide range of variables, for example, by
access route, area and type of property required.

In **Sheffield City Council**, lettings from the housing register are carried out at 22 area offices. A wide range of functions are carried out by the rehousing services section, based centrally, including the development of policies and procedures, monitoring of lettings and authorisation of discretionary decisions, maintenance of the housing register and nominations. Visits to applicants with medical needs are carried out by a centrally-based medical visiting team. Allocations to homeless households are made by a central homelessness section. Marketing campaigns and fast-track lettings are carried out by the housing help desk, again centrally-based. The housing register includes transfers and can be sorted by area, estate and property type. If there is no waiting list for an individual property, housing officers are able to consult neighbouring lists.

2.4 The extent of change

All 65 organisations responding to the random survey were asked if changes had been made to aspects of their lettings policy since the implementation of the Housing Act 1996. The responses are shown in Table 2.1.

TABLE 2.1   Changes in lettings policies since implementation of the Housing Act 1996

Area of change	Yes		No		Don't know/ No answer		Total	
	No.	%	No.	%	No.	%	No.	%
Criteria or weighting of housing need factors	36	55	24	37	5	8	65	100
Those excluded from the housing register	30	46	32	49	3	5	65	100
How transfer applications are processed/ priority given	25	38	36	55	4	6	65	100
Extent of use of local lettings policies	11	17	50	77	4	6	65	100
How applications are processed/ priority given	31	48	28	43	6	9	65	100

Source: Random sample survey responses

Note: Percentages may not total 100 due to rounding

Of the 36 organisations which had made changes in housing need criteria since the implementation of the Housing Act 1996 (or the weighting given to different factors), only five had introduced a completely new system, while 19 had carried out a review of the existing points system. Three organisations had made changes in response to the Housing Act 1996, six had made changes to the weighting given to homeless applicants, and two changed the weighting given to vulnerable or potentially homeless applicants.

Nine of the 30 organisations which had made changes to their exclusions policy were introducing such a policy for the first time. Four had introduced exclusion policies specifically to deal with anti-social behaviour. Six had undertaken a major review of their exclusions policy and four had made minor changes to their policy.

The survey found that 11 organisations had changed the extent to which they used local lettings policies. Five of these had increased the level of scrutiny of applicants in areas where local lettings schemes were in operation.

At the time of the survey, a significant number of the 65 organisations were planning reviews or changes to one or more elements of their lettings policy. The survey found that 14 organisations were planning changes to the housing need criteria they took account of within their lettings policy, 13 to their exclusions policies, eight to the way transfer applicants are dealt with or prioritised, seven to how homeless applicants are dealt with or prioritised, and one to the extent of use of local lettings.

This level of change was mirrored by the case study organisations. Of the five, Lewisham had recently carried out an extensive review of its lettings policy, Notting Hill Housing Trust was in the process of carrying out a review and Sheffield City Council was intending to undertake a review during 2000. In addition, Notting Hill Housing Trust was part of a best value pilot study on 'unjamming the transfer queue' which involved changes in the priority accorded to internal transfer applicants.

It is important to consider the scale of the many changes which have taken (and are taking) place. Table 2.2 shows the changes implemented in the 40 organisations identified from the random and innovation surveys. This shows that a significant minority of organisations have put new approaches in place across a significant proportion of their stock.

TABLE 2.2   Scale of new approaches

Scale	No. of organisations	Per cent
Small number of specific estates/ areas (up to five)	19	42
Significant number of estates/ areas (more than five)	12	26
All estates (not scattered properties)	1	2
Proportion of properties across whole of stock	9	20
Whole stock	1	2
All new developments (RSLs)	4	9

Note: Some organisations were implementing more than one 'new approach'

Motivations for change

There were some differences of opinion between the national organisations interviewed as to what was motivating social landlords to make changes in their lettings policies. One view was that local authorities were starting to make changes as a response to the Government's social exclusion and welfare to work agenda, seeking to tackle unpopular estates and trying to reduce the concentration of disadvantage in the most deprived areas. Another view was that crime and disorder and low demand were the most important factors in stimulating change by registered social landlords. This was supported to some extent in the research, in that RSLs responding to the random survey had more frequently adopted exclusions for anti-social behaviour than responding local authorities. A further factor which was seen as important was an increasing recognition of housing applicants as consumers who should have some choice, or at least be able to express clear preferences and have notice taken of them.

As noted above, 36 organisations responding to the random survey had changed their lettings policy with regard to housing needs criteria in the period since the implementation of the Housing Act 1996. Of these, 17 stated that the changes were made in response to the new legislation, 11 said they were a response to internal change within the organisation and six said they were a response to external change. Over half of the 30 organisations which had made changes to their exclusions policies said that the change was in response to the Housing Act 1996.

There were differences between local authorities and RSLs in the motivation for changes in policy. Local authorities were primarily motivated to change as a result of the Housing Act 1996 while RSLs seem to have been motivated more by internal change within their organisation. However, these two factors are not totally unconnected and the possible influence of the Housing Act 1996 on changes made by registered social landlords should not be ruled out.

The motivation for changes made by the five case study organisations included legislative requirements, but strong themes emerged in response to a number of factors. These include: changing demand for social housing: the experience of communities in which certain types of households with particular needs or housing histories have become concentrated: the needs of existing tenants as well as new applicants; and demands created by regeneration initiatives.

What is changing?

From an analysis of both the random and innovation surveys, it was possible to identify a number of new approaches to lettings which involved one or more of the following:

- changes (increase and decreases) in the extent to which exclusions and/or suspensions of applicants were used
- widening the range of applicants from which lettings could be made
- speeding up the process and reducing bureaucracy
- changes in the degree of scrutiny applied to applications
- applying different criteria to the assessment and prioritisation of applicants with the aim of getting a different mix of tenants
- relaxing eligibility rules so that households can under-occupy properties
- the amount of officer discretion in decisions about lettings.

One or more of these approaches had been implemented by 40 local authorities RSLs responding to the random and innovation surveys as indicated in Table 2.3. The change put in place by most organisations was applying different criteria to the assessment and prioritisation of applicants, while the change put in place by fewest organisations was a decrease in exclusions. Approaches which seek to widen the range of applicants and those which enhance landlord discretion also ranked highly.

TABLE 2.3   Changes in lettings policies

Area of change	No. of organisations
Applying different criteria to assessment and prioritisation of applicants	36
Widening the range of potential applicants	21
More officer discretion	18
Under-occupation	16
Speeding up the process	8
More scrutiny of applicants	6
More exclusions	6
Less scrutiny of applicants	5
Less discretion	3
Less exclusions	2

Source: Random and innovation survey responses - 40 in total

It was also possible to identify whether:

- the motive for the various changes was proactive (in five cases) or reactive (29) or both (four)

- the approach was part of other initiatives such as housing management (three), area regeneration (six) or others (two)

- the approach was applied to all of the stock (one), was area-based (28), individual property/street based (five), or a combination of these (four)

- the approaches were being applied indefinitely (29), as a pilot (three), until the problem was resolved (four), or a combination of these (two)

- other landlords working in the area were taking the same approach to allocations (four).

The examples below indicate that in practice many organisations were incorporating a variety of approaches within a single policy.

Suffolk Heritage Housing Association had a local lettings policy which was used on one estate described by the landlord as being on a 'downward spiral'. The policy involved:

- always making first offers of flats on the estate to people over 40 (applying different criteria)
- not rehousing people with a known history of anti-social behaviour (restricting access)
- relaxing income and capital limits (widening the range of potential applicants).

Nottingham City Council had local lettings policies in place in two areas in which:

- household type/property type matching rules were disregarded (under-occupation)
- lettings were made from different categories of applicant/access routes (different mix)
- there was more scrutiny of applicants and applicants could be excluded as a result of the information gained (more scrutiny linked to more exclusions).

Riverside Housing Association had a local lettings policy in place in an area with a concentration of rehabilitated properties which included conversions of large houses to flats. The policy involved:

- applicants being vetted by the police for any record of drug offences (more scrutiny)
- allocating to fewer single parent families (different mix)
- reconversion of some flats into larger units to enable lettings to two parent families (different mix).

From these and the other approaches used by the 40 local authorities and registered social landlords, it is possible to identify three underlying themes which have clear resonance with the themes emanating from Government. These themes are:

- restricting access to certain groups through the use of exclusions
- opening up access to 'non-traditional' groups
- seeking to develop or create more sustainable communities in areas of social housing.

The next section of this chapter looks in more detail at these themes.

2.5 Restricting access: the use of exclusions

Although only eight of the 40 organisations which had put new approaches in place
involved a change in the use of exclusions, of the 65 organisations responding to the
random survey, only four had a totally open housing register. Table 2.4 shows the
variety of exclusions in place amongst the 65 local authorities and registered social
landlords and their prevalence at the time of the survey. The most common
categories of exclusion related to debts from current or previous social housing
tenancies (49 per cent) and the behaviour of applicants in previous tenancies (48
per cent).

TABLE 2.4   Categories of exclusion

Type of exclusion	Yes		No		DK/Not provided		Total	
	No.	%	No.	%	No.	%	No.	%
Tenant debt	32	49	29	45	4	6	65	100
Ex-tenant behaviour	31	48	24	37	10	15	65	100
Ex-tenant debt	30	46	26	40	9	14	65	100
Age	29	45	27	42	9	14	65	100
Local connections	27	42	35	54	3	5	65	100
Tenant behaviour	27	41	33	51	5	8	65	100
Violence towards staff	23	35	38	59	4	6	65	100
Other	37	57	20	31	8	12	65	100

Source: Random sample survey responses – 38 local authorities and
27 registered social landlords.

Note: Percentages may not total 100 due to rounding

As shown in Table 2.5, RSLs more commonly excluded applicants than local
authorities in all the categories identified except local connection and 'other'.

TABLE 2.5   Categories of exclusion by organisational type

	Local authorities			RSLs		
	Yes %	No %	D/K %	Yes %	No %	D/K %
Local connections	63	32	5	11	85	4
Ex-tenant behaviour	47	40	13	48	30	22
Age	42	42	16	48	37	15
Tenant debt	40	50	11	63	33	4
Tenant behaviour	40	53	8	44	48	7
Ex-tenant debt	40	47	13	59	26	15
Violence towards staff	24	68	8	52	41	7
Other	58	32	11	56	33	11

Source: Random sample survey responses – 38 local authorities
and 27 registered social landlords

Debt

Two organisations stated that they included council tax debt as a reason for
excluding applicants from the housing register, while 26 out of the 32 organisations
which excluded for current tenant debt and 24 out of the 30 organisations which
excluded for ex-tenant debt specified that only housing debt would be taken into
consideration.

When organisations were asked how an excluded applicant with tenant or ex-tenant
debt could get access to the housing register, responses were given as shown in
Table 2.6.

Table 2.6　Applicants with debt - action needed to be taken to gain access to the
housing register/waiting list

Action required	Tenant debt		Ex-tenant debt	
	No.	%	No.	%
Rent arrears cleared	14	44	7	23
Flexible depending on individual circumstances	10	31	8	26
Agreement kept for 'reasonable' period	4	13	4	13
Agreement kept for specified period	3	9	1	3
Not specified	1	3	11	36
Total	32	100	31	100

Source: Random sample survey responses

Anti-social behaviour

Organisations that excluded on the basis of tenant or ex-tenant behaviour were
asked for details of the type of behaviour that was considered as anti-social and
the level of proof required for the decision to exclude an applicant. Table 2.7 shows
that a minority of organisations required a legal stage in possession proceedings to
have been reached, while a majority of organisations had a policy which left this
open to interpretation, or did not specify the types of behaviour which should be
taken into consideration.

TABLE 2.7　Exclusions on the basis of anti-social behaviour:
types of behaviour and level of proof

Type of behaviour	Tenant behaviour		Ex-tenant behaviour	
	No.	%	No.	%
Unspecified/open to interpretation	14	52	18	58
Possession Order/eviction for anti-social behaviour	8	30	11	36
Notice Seeking Possession for anti-social behaviour	4	15	1	3
Level of complaints	1	4	1	3

Source: Random sample survey responses

Age

Almost 45 per cent of organisations in the random sample excluded 16- and 17-year-olds. All of the 29 organisations which excluded applicants on the basis of age excluded young people aged 16 and 17. Of these, 18 said that they would accept applicants of 16 and 17 years of age if they had a rent guarantor or if a social services support package was in place.

Local connection

Local authorities were more likely than RSLs to restrict access on the grounds that the applicant did not have a local connection. Of the 27 organisations that operated local connection criteria for access to the housing register, 24 were local authorities, and of the remaining three, two were large scale voluntary transfer housing associations. Of these 27, 20 operated a residence qualification and five a connection through work or support needs. The use of residence requirements by neighbouring authorities has been flagged by some authorities, (for example, Bristol City Council and the London Borough of Camden), as having a direct detrimental impact on their ability to meet housing need by increasing the level of demand they experience for their housing, although others say they have no proof that such policies applied in neighbouring authorities increase demand in their area.

Other reasons for excluding applicants

Of the 65 organisations in the random survey, 37 stated that they operated exclusions for other reasons. The categories identified are shown in Table 2.8.

TABLE 2.8   Other reasons for exclusions

Exclusion	No.	%
Immigration status	14	38
Sufficient income/capital to meet need	13	35
Owner-occupation	12	32
Criminal conviction	9	24
Owed duty by another LA	7	19
Existing LA/RSL tenant	6	16
Fraudulent application	2	5
Eviction for fraudulent application	2	5
Member of household on transfer list	1	3
Member of forces not resident for 2 years prior to applying	1	3

Source: Random sample survey responses

Ten had an exclusions policy for applicants with criminal convictions. The range of convictions relating to exclusion was wide but covered most serious offences: sex offences, arson, murder and physical assault. There was also a range of approaches to dealing with these offences, from blanket bans on applicants with specific convictions, to deferring applicants.

Little was said about statutory exclusions relating to the asylum and immigration status of applicants and this was only mentioned by 14 of the 65 organisations as a reason for excluding applicants.

In addition to exclusions policies, suspension policies were operated by 51 of the 65 organisations. The majority of these identified debt as the main reason for suspensions, although three also identified refusal of offers as a reason. In the majority of cases, suspensions because of outstanding debt remained in force until the debt had been cleared, although a number of organisations were willing to reinstate an applicant if a repayment arrangement had been adhered to for some time. From the organisation's policy documents, it was possible to identify a further 14 that used suspension from the waiting list as a penalty for refusing a specified number of reasonable offers.

Monitoring of exclusions

Although only four of the 65 organisations responding to the random survey had totally open waiting lists, just one third of them undertook any monitoring of exclusions such as the number of applicants excluded and reasons. Most (57) of the organisations had an appeals procedure in place for those applicants that had been excluded.

The approach of the five case study organisations to exclusions and suspensions is summarised below.

CDS Housing accepted applications from anyone over the age of 16. Nobody was directly excluded from the list but negative points were used in response to certain behaviour or circumstances. These included serious breach of tenancy or physical violence to staff or tenants within the last two years and cases where an applicant or immediate family member owes money to CDS. In addition those with equity of £25,000 and applying for general needs housing (£35,000 if applying for sheltered housing) and applicants evicted from a registered social landlord in the last two years, were negatively pointed.

The London Borough of Lewisham accepted applications from those who had been continuously resident in the borough 12 months prior to their application, although the applicant had to be a 'qualifying person' within the meaning of section 161 of the Housing Act 1996. This, of course, was no guarantee of an offer of rehousing. The authority considered the exclusions categories 'too crude' to be applied and accepted applications on the register whatever their previous housing record. However, council tenants in rent arrears would not be

---

made an offer of rehousing while they had an outstanding debt. While the 1996
Act removed any duty on local authorities to offer permanent housing to priority
homeless households, it did not remove the right. As far as possible such
households had been given reasonable preference when lettings were made
from the register.

At the time of the study, there were over 400 asylum seekers in Lewisham
dependent on temporary accommodation and subsistence payments. Where
they get 'leave to remain', families were likely to be given tenancies in
temporary accommodation and single people were expected to find housing in
the private sector, although once 'leave to remain' has been granted they have
similar rights under the homelessness legislation as other applicants.

Notting Hill Housing Trust did not have its own waiting list for new applicants,
but did have an internal transfer list. The organisation did not exclude transfer
applicants for arrears, but used suspensions. If there was a history of nuisance
or threats being made to staff, applicants were excluded. This happened rarely,
but in the past ex-tenants with these histories had been nominated to the
organisation by local authorities. The trust excluded applicants where a tenancy
was seen as being unsustainable. This was judged on a case specific basis. The
exclusions policies of the local authorities which nominated to the organisation
were felt to have more of an impact than the trust's own policy.

Former housing debts were a major issue for **Rochdale MBC**. If a debt did not
exceed £250, applicants could be rehoused through Selectahome (fast-track
route) although they were expected to pay off the debt, with the agreement to
clear arrears becoming part of their tenancy agreement. If the debt exceeded
£250, applicants had to go through the mainstream lettings system. Whether
the applicant was excluded or not depended on the amount of the debt,
circumstances surrounding how the debt arose, their level of housing need and
willingness to repay the debt. In reality, exclusions for debt were much more
likely in high-demand areas. Applicants could also be excluded on the basis of
previous serious anti-social behaviour, for example, cases which had been taken
to court and cases involving violence towards staff. Although there was no
formal rule, the authority was reluctant to exclude anyone on the basis of anti-
social behaviour that had occurred more than two years prior to the rehousing
application. Rochdale would exclude 16- and 17-year-olds if they felt that they
did not have the resources or support to sustain a tenancy. The council
monitored the number and type of exclusions and had done this since the
implementation of the Housing Act 1996, although exclusions on the grounds of
neighbour nuisance had been monitored for longer than this. In 1998/99, there
were a total of 526 non-qualifying persons, compared to 506 in 1997/98.

Sheffield City Council operated an open housing register, with only statutory
exclusions applied. People from outside of Sheffield could apply and very few
exclusions were applied locally. However, suspensions from the housing register
were used extensively, particularly for rent arrears. Applicants who owed rent

arrears or any other money to the housing revenue account would not be offered rehousing until they had cleared the debt or had maintained a repayment agreement for a significant period of time. There were exceptions for people with urgent housing need, including homeless households and a framework for making discretionary decisions was in place. Applications would also be suspended if the applicant had refused two offers; if the applicant had not kept the council property where they were the tenant in a satisfactory condition; or if the applicant was a former Sheffield City Council tenant who had been evicted for nuisance or harassment. In March 1999, there were 16,247 households with active applications on Sheffield's housing register, while 53,439 applications were suspended for various reasons. This figure includes applicants who did not want to be considered for rehousing for the time being. A report in 2000 said that the city had concluded that it has an excess supply over demand of 20,000 homes (Bramley et al, 2000).

Impact of exclusions

Housing debt and anti-social behaviour were identified from the random survey as the most common type of exclusion. However, there appear to be great differences in the responses of local authorities and registered social landlords to the opportunity of excluding people with debt or a history of anti-social behaviour from registering their housing need. Some will take the opportunity to exclude outright, while others have a more open housing register but apply some sort of penalty to certain applicants, for example, by the use of negative points or suspension. Sheffield City Council considered that it was preferable to register people with housing debt, but suspend them to encourage them to pay so that they could be rehoused. The negative points approach taken by CDS Housing meant that applicants with high levels of housing need could still be rehoused even if they had arrears or a history of anti-social behaviour.

It is of continuing concern that, despite advice to the contrary, local authorities and registered social landlords which exclude applicants from their housing registers do not routinely monitor the numbers and reasons for exclusion.

2.6 Opening up access to a wider range of applicants

Of the 40 organisations which had put new approaches in place, 21 had sought to widen the range of potential applicants for their housing. This was mirrored by the response to the random survey in which 24 of the 65 organisations responding to the random survey said that they made some attempt to attract non-traditional groups to apply for their housing. Of these, 14 were local authorities and ten were RSLs.

The breakdown of these by region is provided in Table 2.9. The results of this survey do not identify a pattern relating the level of demand in a region to the proportion of organisations which have tried to attract non-traditional groups. However, the sample sizes are very small at the regional level.

TABLE 2.9   Attracting non-traditional groups to apply for housing

Region	Yes		No		No information	
	No.	%	No.	%	No.	%
North	4	6				
North West	5	8	4	6		
Yorkshire/ Humberside	3	5				
East Midlands	1	2	6	9		
West Midlands	2	3	1	2		
South West	2	3	5	8		
East Anglia	1	2	3	5		
South East	6	9	8	12	1	2
London	3	5	10	15		
Totals	24	37	40	62	1	2

Source: Random sample survey responses

Note: Percentages do not add to 100 due to rounding

The most common method by which local authorities and registered social landlords were attempting to attract non-traditional groups was advertising. One of the key groups which was being targeted was people in employment. Some brief examples are provided below.

South Yorkshire Housing Association had been working with Rotherham District Council to develop a local lettings policy to broaden the base of applicants to include more applicants who were young and in employment. Methods used were advertising in the local press and 'to let' notices placed in the windows of properties available for letting. The association had a reasonable response to the advertisements and had let some properties as a result of the 'to let' notices.

Sanctuary Housing Association had used advertising for a block of flats which had been refurbished and had a concierge scheme in place. Estate agent type advertisements had been placed in local newspapers to raise the profile of the properties. Potential applicants were able to visit the scheme before it was ready to let. The block of flats was let to a very mixed population, from people earning a 'reasonable' income to lone parent families on benefits.

Both Family Housing Association (Manchester) and Birmingham City Council noted that they tried to attract black and minority ethnic groups who had not traditionally applied for social housing and used information targeted specifically at these groups. Targets were set to reflect the ethnic mix of the areas in which properties were being let.

The above examples of advertising and marketing were relatively small-scale. Three of the five case study organisations had also carried out marketing of their properties. One of these was marketing related to more than one area (CDS Housing), while two involved marketing strategies for a significant proportion or the whole of the organisation's stock (Sheffield and Rochdale). Brief summaries of these approaches are provided below.

Sheffield City Council: housing help desk

The help desk aimed to provide an accessible service, clear information, and a fast track through the application process. The help desk team in the central office of the authority carried out a number of functions, including widespread advertising for local authority housing, both general campaigns and those targeted at specific groups such as students.

Applicants could register on the same day that they made an enquiry. Help desk staff discussed waiting times for different properties, advised applicants and liaised with area offices on behalf of the applicant. In some cases, an applicant could enquire, register, view properties and sign up on the same day. Applicants did not have to be in housing need as determined by the points system used by Sheffield for mainstream allocations.

Area offices could give the help desk keys of properties for which there was no waiting list and the help desk would promote the property and carry out the allocation. Area offices could also ask the help desk to provide details of potential applicants for properties which had been refused by people on the waiting list and/or for which there was no waiting list left. In these cases, the area offices would carry out the allocation. The help desk could also be used to build up a waiting list for any property with a waiting list of 12 months or less.

Rochdale Metropolitan Borough Council: Selectahome

The main purpose of the Selectahome scheme was to provide applicants with an offer of accommodation within 24 hours of an application. The scheme was designed to be as accessible as possible. Rehousing officers emphasised the choices that were available to applicants, rather than placing hurdles in their way. The scheme relied more on verbal contact than on paperwork, and had its own hotline with a different number from the council number. The aim was to provide as much choice as possible and applicants were usually offered several properties. However, properties which were let through the scheme were unpopular, so they were predominantly flats and properties in less attractive areas.

The needs of applicants were not assessed in any systematic way – Selectahome was the opposite of a needs-based system. A mixture of different types of applicant applied via Selectahome, from homeless households, to those without any specific housing needs, but who wished to move.

Impact of opening up access

There is an inevitable tension between opening up access for social housing and continuing to meet the housing needs of the most vulnerable people in society, as indeed there is a tension between addressing needs and the use of exclusion polices. This tension is not as great where there is low demand for at least some of the housing stock. Where this is the case in Sheffield and Rochdale, a needs-based points system runs alongside a more market-based approach.

2.7 Towards more sustainable communities

The aim of creating or developing sustainable communities underpinned a wide variety of policies which had been put in place by the 40 social landlords identified from the random and innovation surveys as having adopted new approaches to allocations. This was also an aim which underpinned many of the changes put in place by the 36 organisations which had adopted new approaches involving different criteria being applied to the assessment and prioritisation of applicants. Specific ways in which organisations aimed at sustainability included:

- setting targets for different groups of applicants or access routes
- under-occupation of family housing to reduce child density
- excluding people with certain characteristics
- housing local people and/or those with a commitment to the area
- the promotion of transfers within estates to support communities
- flexible policies which could be adapted to the needs of different areas.

While it is not always clear what constitutes a sustainable community, brief examples of the different ways individual organisations are trying to address the issue are given below.

Setting targets

A number of organisations had set targets for lettings to new developments to ensure a good 'mix' of applicants. Epsom and Ewell District Council set specific targets for lettings to a new development built in conjunction with two RSLs. These included targets for people in employment and the total number of children.

Under-occupation

Aldwyck Housing Association's policy in areas of difficult-to-let housing involved making lettings to applicants who would not normally have had priority for the type of property. For example, single people were allocated two-bedroom houses. This also had a role in reducing child density.

Exclusion

Exclusion of people with certain characteristics was thought to help community sustainability. Newcastle and Whiteley Housing Association put a common lettings policy in place with two partner RSLs which excluded applicants with a history of crime and anti-social behaviour.

Local people

Some approaches gave priority to local people and/or people who would be committed to living in the area. In Manchester, Family Housing Association's local lettings policy targeted applicants with a commitment to the area and excluded those with no local connection.

Promoting transfers

The London Borough of Lewisham's estate transfer scheme enabled Lewisham tenants to move within or between 16 selected estates throughout the borough, to property of the size and type they needed, whether or not they would otherwise be eligible for an offer. The estate transfer scheme was designed to offer transfers to tenants who wanted to move to more suitable property while staying within their estate, or any of the other estates within the scheme. Tenants could move whether or not they have enough points for a transfer anywhere else. The scheme was specifically designed to help promote community stability. These issues are considered more fully in Chapter 3.

Flexible lettings policies

Bradford and Northern Housing Association had introduced flexibility into its corporate lettings policy so that local policies could take account of local issues such as high child density.

Applicant choice

Previous research has emphasised that the degree of choice for residents (in moving to a certain property in a given area) is more important than the notion of a 'socially balanced' community which would automatically be successful (Cole et al, 1996). The traditional way in which applicant choice is considered is how readily applicants can express their preferences and how many offers of accommodation they can receive before any penalties are imposed. This is in the context of properties being 'allocated' by officers within local authorities and RSLs.

TABLE 2.10 Extent to which applicants are given preference

	Yes		No		Don't know		Not specified		Information not provided		Total	
	No.	%	No.	%	No.	%	No.	%	No.	%	No.	%
Location	22	34	2	3	6	9	16	25	19	29	65	100
Property type	4	6	19	29	4	6	18	28	20	31	65	100
Size	2	3	22	34	3	5	18	28	20	31	65	100

Source: Random sample survey responses

The survey found that 27 organisations placed a limit on the number of offers an applicant was allowed, with five allowing only one offer, 14 allowing two and three allowing three. All but one of the 27 imposed a penalty for the refusal of reasonable offers beyond the limit. The most common penalty was a period of suspension from the housing register/waiting list during which time no offers of accommodation would be made. Eight of the organisations removed applicants from the housing register altogether, with two specifying a waiting period before reapplying.

> The case study organisations took the following approaches to offers and applicant choice.
>
> Among the 65 organisations responding to the random survey, the extent to which applicants were given the opportunity to state their preferences for location, property type and size of property varied considerably as shown in Table 2.10.
>
> The choice available to CDS Housing applicants depended on the availability of property and the applicants' eligibility for their chosen areas. The main choices were by location and property type. Applicants could

stipulate as many location preferences as they wanted, but for the more popular areas, applicants would not be allowed on the list if they did not reach the designated points threshold. In difficult-to-let areas, the policy allowed for under-occupation, so that smaller households have more choice in these areas.

There was no limit on offers for applicants to Rochdale except for applicants coming through the homeless route who were allowed one reasonable offer only. There were no limits on offers for applicants coming through the Selectahome (fast track) route.

In Sheffield City Council, housing register applicants had two offers and homeless applicants one. There were no limits on the number of offers which could be made to applicants by the help desk (fast track route).

The overt marketing approach used by Sheffield and Rochdale enabled applicants to opt themselves in when they were interested in one or more properties rather than be allocated the property. This approach also allowed applicants to view more than one property at a time and did not impose any penalties for refusals. However, properties let in this way were not in high demand from applicants on the housing register.

2.8 Conclusions

The research has shown that over half of our sampled social landlords had made changes to their needs criteria since the Housing Act 1996, while almost half had changed their policies on exclusions (including a significant proportion which had introduced them for the first time). Almost 40 per cent had changed the way they dealt with transfer applicants while nearly half had changed how homeless applications were processed. Nearly 20 per cent reported changes to the use of local lettings policies. In addition, a significant number of others reported further planned changes.

A number of key themes underpinning change were identified. These included: changing demand for social housing; meeting the needs of existing tenants as well as new applicants; the experience of communities where previous policies had resulted in over-concentrations of particular types of households; concern about the role of lettings in creating sustainable communities; and demand generated by regeneration initiatives.

Despite advice to the contrary, local authorities and RSLs which exclude applicants from their housing registers do not routinely monitor the numbers and reasons for exclusion.

Chapter 3:

Local lettings and the use of transfers

3.1 Introduction

In Chapter 2 it was noted that lettings are often a compromise between a number of different objectives such as giving priority to those in greatest housing need, letting properties quickly, satisfying applicant preferences, being cost effective and achieving a high degree of consistency and fairness in the treatment of individual applicants. Over a long period there has been a broad consensus that awarding priority to those in the most severe housing need should be of paramount importance.

However, during the 1990s arguments have emerged that letting policies should also seek to promote more cohesive and settled communities. This objective, it is suggested, should not replace other key objectives such as meeting priority need, but feature as a legitimate additional consideration. At the same time, many social landlords see lettings in a more strategic context than being just about meeting priority housing need. Indeed, some years ago the Audit Commission (1992) urged local authorities to adopt a more strategic approach to their activities, including lettings. Thus, whilst lettings may be driven by a desire to rehouse people in priority housing need, there is also an aim to provide a responsive service which takes account of applicants' preferences as well as their needs. It has been argued elsewhere that social sector tenants should enjoy the same opportunities as others to exercise some degree of choice, and policies which artificially restrict the mobility of existing tenants are unlikely to be successful in the long term. Those who are able to may leave the sector and those who are not are likely to become very dissatisfied (Griffiths et al, 1997).

3.2 How widespread are local lettings policies?

Research has shown that, at a local level, lettings policies can be either part of the problem of difficult-to-let and difficult-to-manage estates, or part of the solution (DoE, 1980). Work by Glennester and Turner (1993) indicated the ways in which placing vulnerable households on estates can undermine the benefits of good local management. Page's work on RSLs similarly drew attention to the ways in which concentrations of disadvantaged households and people under stress (as well as high child densities) on new estates could lead to a rapid spiral of decline (Page, 1993). In his subsequent work he argued that, despite the pressures of housing need, there were many ways, such as mixed tenure, internal transfers, dwelling mix, and under-letting, in which RSLs should let new estates more creatively to produce more varied local communities (Page, 1994).

However, while there have been growing concerns with the search for so-called 'balanced communities', often within specific tenures as well as mixed tenure communities, the definition of a 'balanced community' has proved extremely elusive (Forrest, 2000). The problem is perhaps less one of household or occupational imbalance and more an issue of lack of employment, poverty, high turnover of tenancies and social exclusion. As such, providers of social housing have been expected to address issues of social exclusion and social polarisation and deal with areas of multiple disadvantage.

Earlier work (Griffiths et al, 1996) analysed the use of local lettings, and showed that they were often used for unpopular estates experiencing severe management problems. Less frequently, they were introduced to influence the social composition of new estates on first letting, and occasionally to protect existing stable communities. This earlier study found that many such schemes had been justified as exceptional and introduced as short-term measures to address problems associated with low demand or to achieve a balance of rehousing for different types of households, often coming through different access channels. Typically they were found to apply to only a small proportion of the housing stock of individual landlords. In most cases such schemes have been developed at the instigation of the landlord, although on occasion tenants have initiated such approaches.

The Social Exclusion Unit report on housing management from policy action team (PAT) 5 (DETR, 1999b) confirmed that social landlords have attempted to sustain or reverse the decline of specific estates by the use of local lettings plans or 'community lettings', which take account of the needs of the area as a whole, as well as the individual needs of applicants. It noted that, whilst the Housing Act 1996 requires local authorities to ensure reasonable preference is given to those in need, there is flexibility within current legislation for letting schemes which promote mixed communities whilst continuing to give priority to those in housing need. The question is to what extent such approaches are being used.

Using the results from the random telephone survey, 19 of the 65 respondents (29 per cent) said they had some form of local lettings policy in place. Of these, almost two-thirds had consulted with other organisations (such as local authorities and tenants' groups) before introducing these schemes, whilst nine said that existing tenants had been involved in either the development or implementation of the new schemes.

This survey is not directly comparable with earlier work (Griffiths et al, 1996), but the indications are that the use of local lettings is now more widespread than was the case in 1995, when only 16 per cent of responding social landlords reported operating local lettings schemes. However, it may be that social landlords are now more willing to admit to the use of modified lettings policies in a climate where issues of changing demand are being discussed openly and where there is evidence of a culture shift in central Government's thinking in relation to the letting and marketing of social housing.

The reasons given for introducing local lettings policies fell into three main categories:

- tackling unpopular estates

- attempting to achieve a balanced community

- maintaining the stability of an established area which is experiencing no problems.

Individual social landlords may have introduced local lettings policies for one or more of these reasons. However, in the majority of cases where they have been introduced, the aim has been to stabilise the local area (58 per cent), with other stated objectives being the reduction of void levels and turnover rates, tackling anti-social behaviour, and the reduction of child densities.

In 11 out of the 19 cases, local lettings policies have involved actively seeking to attract new types of applicant (for example, childless couples, mature or older households and the economically active). All 19 organisations which reported operating local lettings policies said that there was a degree of officer discretion allowed within the process.

Within the organisations which reported operating local lettings policies, there appeared to be little systematic evaluation of these policies, although four had only recently introduced such policies and were therefore not in a position to comment on evaluation (although it is appropriate to put monitoring arrangements in place at the outset). Only one organisation said it intended to undertake a specific evaluation of its local lettings policy. Five others pointed to the use of housing management statistics (such as void levels, turnover rates, and reported nuisance complaints) as the means of evaluating the success or failure of local policies. The general lack of monitoring of local lettings policies against set objectives is cause for concern if individual social landlords are to evaluate how successful such schemes have been, what benefits have been achieved, and at what cost.

3.3 Local lettings and low demand

It was noted in Chapter 1 that there has been considerable analysis of the changing nature and pattern of demand for social rented housing (Cole et al, 1999; Holmans and Simpson, 1999; Murie et al, 1998), as well as consideration of the implications for policy and appropriate responses. The Government has published its own report into unpopular housing which found that the North West, North East and Yorkshire and Humberside regions have the highest concentrations of unpopular housing, but that even in high demand areas there may be pockets of unpopular housing, often of a specific type or design or in poor condition (DETR, 1999d). The PAT 7 report on unpopular housing made a number of specific recommendations designed to address the problem of stigma in relation to some social housing, specifically by aiming to introduce a more mixed income occupancy into the most unpopular estates and giving greater choice to those accessing social housing.

The PAT 7 report argued that it was essential to make some changes to current lettings policies, and made the following recommendations:

- the DETR and the Housing Corporation should develop for consultation proposals to provide local authorities and RSLs with the power in clearly defined circumstances to grant assured shorthold tenancies (recommendation 34). It was argued that letting schemes designed to attract tenants with low housing need priority should not necessarily provide all the benefits (for example, the right to buy) which go with a secure tenancy.

- the DETR should promote pilots in local authorities experiencing low demand to release a proportion of new lettings through an advertising scheme (recommendation 35). The Housing Green Paper confirmed the Government's intention in this respect (DETR/DSS, 2000a).

- the DETR should discuss with local government ways in which 'local connection' requirements for access to social rented housing can be relaxed to ensure the best use of housing where there is a high demand for local authority or RSL stock (recommendation 36). The report argued that 'local connection' qualifications become meaningless in areas of low demand and can inhibit the best use of the stock in high-demand areas.

As we noted in section 3.2 above, the most frequently cited reason for introducing local lettings policies related to unpopular and low demand stock, with changes to the lettings policies often being introduced as part of a package of measures to try to address the problem.

As we illustrated in Chapter 1, in examining HIP data in relation to difficult-to-let housing, almost all social landlords have some low-demand properties or estates, even in areas of otherwise high housing need. In such cases it is not unusual for social landlords to introduce flexibility into the lettings system through the use of additional criteria within the normal policy or the introduction of a specific scheme outside of the normal policy.

In order to tackle perceived problems of low demand, a number of different approaches may be used. For example, targets or quotas may be used across a

range of household attributes to avoid concentrations of highly disadvantaged or
vulnerable groups such as homeless households or lone parent families. Efforts may
also be made to reduce child densities, perhaps by relaxing the normal bedroom
standards so as to allow under-occupation and to widen eligibility for individual
vacancies.

Sheffield City Council introduced a local lettings policy in respect of five roads
on one estate in December 1994. The policy involved relaxing eligibility criteria
for three bedroom properties and awarding extra points for applicants with a
close relative living in the area (although extra points were not awarded if the
current tenant was subject to a notice of intention of seeking possession or a
court order for nuisance). However, there was little take-up of the extra points
and the scheme was not extended.

Elsewhere in the city, on two other estates (both non-traditional housing,
and in very low demand), the eligibility criteria for different property types have
been relaxed so that single people can be allocated two-bedroom properties.
It was suggested that this practice should be extended in these areas, so that a
single person or couple could be allocated three bedroom accommodation.
This might help community stability, since the council was not always able to
rehouse someone near to their family because of ineligibility for particular
property types.

Sheffield has also designated blocks of flats for particular age groups, although
there is flexibility for redesignation and tenants are involved.

Alternatively, or additionally, some schemes introduced in areas of low demand have
been linked to paying more attention to individual lettings at the outset. The aims
are: to ensure that applicants will be able to maintain a tenancy; to ensure that
those with a known history of anti-social behaviour are excluded; and (more
positively) to give a degree of priority to those who really want to be housed in a
particular area. In some cases lettings policies are supported by more active and
widespread marketing of rehousing opportunities (sometimes anonymously, without
identifying schemes as being social housing), by using incentives (for example, the
provision of furnished tenancies) to encourage the take-up of tenancies and then by
making residents feel that they belong once they have moved in. CDS Housing's use
of neighbourhood housing plans is an example of a wide-ranging approach to the
letting of property in areas of low demand.

CDS Housing operates two local lettings schemes called neighbourhood housing plans (NHPs), Introduced in January 1999, they cover two estates, one in Liverpool 8 (Windermere Green - an ex-Liverpool city council estate) and the other Castlefield in Runcorn (an estate transferred to CDS in 1989 from the New Town Development Corporation).

The NHPs were introduced for a number of reasons. In addition to seeking to address high turnover, a reduced demand and the disproportionate number of disadvantaged applicants, the schemes also had wider intentions in aiming to address the general decline in the area, to improve the tenure mix and tackle crime. The objectives of the NHPs are:

- **to raise the profile and improve the image of the area**
- **to have a positive impact on the social and physical environment**
- **to increase demand for properties, particularly for those with a commitment to the area**
- **to reduce the turnover of tenancies, through sensitive lettings and positive housing management initiatives**
- **to make properties as attractive as possible to prospective tenants**
- **to establish and support residents' groups, and make positive contacts with other organisations in the area.**

Allocation policies in the NHPs are based on CDS Housing's general lettings policy, but additional points are awarded for specific criteria including local connection, economic activity and age (over 40). The NHPs have five main components: sustaining tenancies; marketing; pre-tenancy work; lettings; and sign-up and post tenancy.

This example illustrates a number of key elements in an approach to lettings in the context of low demand. Firstly, it emphasises the importance of pre-tenancy checks, as a means of identifying support needs among new tenants. This means there has to be close cooperation (and sharing of information) between social landlords and other statutory and voluntary sector service providers so that needs identified can be addressed. In seeking to attract a wider range of applicants there is also a need to change the culture of staff working within social landlord organisations, shifting the emphasis from acting as gatekeepers within a bureaucracy to one in which customer service is the highest priority. Secondly, it emphasises a degree of flexibility within allocation policies. Thirdly, it illustrates the value of advice and information given to tenants at the start of, and during the early stages of, a new tenancy.

3.4 Local lettings and stabilising communities

In some instances local lettings policies have been introduced, not only to address problems of low demand, but also to stabilise local communities by reducing the turnover of tenancies.

In 1997 Sheffield City Council introduced a six-month pilot programme to provide furnished accommodation, and this has now been extended so that it covers 200 properties. The majority of people living in these properties are aged between 18 and 24 years old and the provision of furniture is funded by a service change. This initiative is seen as a way of stabilising the community. Prior to the introduction of furnished tenancies, the average length of tenancy was three to four months. Now it is nine to 12 months, and there are some young people who have been living in the properties since the start of the pilot. Previously people were choosing to live in the private rented sector no matter how bad the condition of the property, because furnished social sector lettings were unavailable.

South Yorkshire Housing Association has developed local lettings on two estates, linked to wider regeneration initiatives. These have been discussed with the council and with local residents. Rehousing priority is being given to people with a local connection to the estates whilst anyone who has previously abandoned property or who has evidence of anti-social behaviour against them (not necessarily an eviction) has been excluded from rehousing.

In a rather different context, Peterborough District Council has introduced a villages policy which gives preference, but not exclusive access, to offers of tenancies to households with a local connection. In such cases the degree of need of the household with a local connection may be less than for lettings in the more urban areas of the district, but the overriding objective is to sustain the local village communities.

3.5 Local lettings and sustainable communities

In some cases local lettings schemes have been developed with a view to creating or maintaining 'balanced' or 'sustainable' communities. The aim is usually to produce a more mixed community than would normally be the case through the traditional letting system. Underpinning this is a general concern about the kind of communities which are being created through the normal system.

In considering the concept of 'balanced' communities, it must be recognised that there is limited scope for social landlords to manipulate social balance through their lettings policies. It may be that developing mixed tenure schemes and attracting a mix of owners and renters may be a more appropriate approach than just amending lettings policies. Meanwhile, if the lettings policy results in the exclusion of particular groups of people from tenancies, a question must be asked: can the community created be described as balanced?

The research identified a number of organisations which had developed local lettings policies with a view to creating a wider social mix or more balanced communities. However, this has been done in a number of ways, and with lettings as part of a wider package.

Bentilee Community Housing Trust, on an estate transfer in Stoke-on-Trent, has introduced a scheme (July 1999) designed to create a more balanced community. Concern had been growing that the estate had become 'ghettoised', so attempts have been made to attract more employed people into the area by setting targets for specific roads and blocks. All tenants are on non-secure starter tenancies for one year, with conversion to an assured tenancy if there are no tenancy problems. The scheme is in place for three years, after which it has to have an approved extension from the Housing Corporation. It is reviewed annually, but it is too early to say whether it is achieving its objectives.

Notting Hill Housing Trust has not been using local lettings policies as defined by the Housing Corporation – that is to say as a tool to regenerate and revitalise areas of decline. Instead they are being used as a stabilising tool to help balance communities in areas of high demand.

The main objective behind the trust's local lettings is to develop estates that are manageable. The aim is to reduce the number of problems on these estates by attempting to adjust the profile of its tenant population. This is not necessarily easy when there are pressures to house those in greatest need, especially from local authorities. Indeed the boroughs with whom the trust works most closely have viewed local lettings with some scepticism and seen them as a means of 'cherry picking' tenants. However, the Trust sees this approach as common sense, following the problems highlighted by the Page report (Page, 1993), and the organisation has asked its partner local authorities to provide a mixed profile of nominations for new developments.

The London Borough of Lewisham has specific local lettings plans for all new build schemes, both under estate action/regeneration (in partnership with Family or Hyde housing associations) and for other RSL new build schemes.

All family housing developed under regeneration schemes is offered first to Lewisham council tenants living within the boundaries of the estate action scheme. This is done in the following order of priority:

- rehousing needs reflected by 200 or more points
- applicants overcrowded by two or more bedrooms (priority by degree of overcrowding)
- medical priority (again in priority order)
- households living in accommodation requiring extensive repairs, where these cannot be done whilst the tenant is in residence
- transfer applicants under-occupying three bedroom properties (or larger)
- those resident on the estate for ten years or more.

A third of the properties not taken up in this way are offered to any Lewisham council tenant approved for rehousing, in points order. The remaining properties are then offered to those on the housing register approved for rehousing, again in points order. Similar arrangements are made in respect of other RSL new build schemes in the borough.

3.6 The role of transfers in the lettings system

Earlier research has shown marked differences in the strategies and procedures adopted by different social landlords in deciding priorities between transfer and waiting list applicants (Maclennan and Kay, 1994). It also pointed to landlords (particularly in southern England) adopting explicit lettings plans and developing transfer-led lettings strategies. Transfers can play a key role in an overall lettings strategy, since they provide the opportunity for creating vacancies of the right size and type in the right locations into which new tenants, often in high housing need, can move (Griffiths et al, 1997). At the same time, unless they are organised and implemented efficiently, an over-emphasis on transfers may add to the time it takes to rehouse new applicants with urgent housing needs, as well as rent loss if properties have to be held vacant to facilitate long chains of moves.

All of our case studies saw transfers as an important means of making the best use of their stock and responding to the changing needs of their tenants. In their general lettings policies some organisations award some categories of points only to transfer applicants. Sheffield, for example, give points to transfer applicants for moves which will release a disabled person's property. They also award specific points to their tenants where they have suffered domestic violence or harassment.

By way of contrast, Notting Hill Housing Trust, while giving priority to certain categories of transfer applicant (harassment cases, medical priorities, under-occupation and decanting), has argued that the current needs of transfer applicants cannot be met. The transfer list is not reducing and transfers have to operate within the constraints of nominations obligations to local authorities. However, there have been moves to be as creative as possible, in some areas using transfers to fill true voids, creating a vacancy chain and using the nomination to fill the resulting end vacancy. This can lead to a better use of the stock, but requires co-operation and flexibility on the part of local authorities. As we noted in the previous section, this may lead to RSLs being accused of 'cherry picking' particular tenants, as well as leaving less desirable vacancies available for the nominee at the end of the chain.

The London Borough of Lewisham operates a number of initiatives which facilitate transfers, without being entirely needs based. Three specific examples are set out below. As we show, none operates on a very large scale, although in aggregate in 1998/99 the three made up a third of all transfers.

• **The estate transfer scheme**

Under this initiative existing Lewisham Council tenants can move within or between 16 selected estates in the Borough, to property of a size and type appropriate for their needs. Priority is given firstly to those under-occupying family-sized property, secondly to those who are overcrowded, and finally to others with rehousing need, in points order. Any bedsits and one-bedroom flats can be let under the scheme, although ground floor flats must first be offered to those with a medical priority for such accommodation.

A quarter of family accommodation can be let under the scheme. Other than in exceptional circumstances tenants in rent arrears, or where the property could not be relet immediately on vacation, are excluded.

In 1998/99 the estate transfer scheme accounted for 31 lettings - 4 per cent of all transfers.

• **Like for like scheme**

The scheme is designed for those tenants who do not have enough points for a transfer, but who want to move to another council property (of similar size and type) elsewhere in the borough. In addition to the criteria set out for the estate transfer scheme, Lewisham tenants also have to have lived at their current address for at least six months and must not be under-occupying.

Under this initiative the offer can only be of the same type as the tenants' present home (or a less desirable type of accommodation, although those in bedsit accommodation can be offered one bed flats). Transfer applicants can be considered for vacancies in any of the neighbourhoods where they may wish to move to, but if the property is needed for an applicant with a higher priority it is awarded to them.

In 1998/99 137 lettings were made under the like for like scheme - 19 per cent of all transfers.

• **Under-occupation scheme**

The scheme attempts to increase the supply of two-, three-, four- and five-bedroom houses, ground floor flats and maisonettes and larger (three-, four, five-bedroom) flats. Transfers can be sanctioned, and reasonable removal expenses paid, even where under-occupying tenants would not otherwise be entitled to a transfer.

The under-occupation scheme resulted in 71 lettings in 1998/99 – 10 per cent of transfers.

3.7 Conclusions

Lettings policies have a role to play in improving and monitoring the quality of life on social housing estates. However, their potential should not be exaggerated. They are one tool in a much broader strategy to address issues of changing demand and expectation and may need to be accompanied by changes in other housing management policies and practices, as well as investment in the physical improvement of the housing stock and its environment.

This chapter has examined the extent to which social landlords are using local lettings policies and their reasons for doing so. The three main reasons are:

- **to tackle unpopular and low-demand properties or estates**

- **attempts to achieve a more sustainable community**

- **the desire to maintain the stability of an established area.**

Where such policies have been introduced, in a majority of cases there has been an accompanying desire to attract new types of applicant, often through the active marketing of properties. In some instances local schemes have also been accompanied by more choice (provision of furnished tenancies, fewer limitations on offers), opportunities for under-occupation, and higher levels of pre and post tenancy housing management services. The widening of access, the moves towards engineering a different mix of types of household and the use of exclusions well illustrate the tensions between giving housing priority to those in the greatest need and not creating concentrations of the most disadvantaged on particular estates.

In some instances the introduction of local lettings policies has also been accompanied by tighter use of selection criteria (for example, local connection) and the wider use of exclusions of particular households. In some cases targets have been set to avoid over-concentration of particular types of households with a view to achieving more sustainable communities.

This chapter has highlighted the contribution which transfers can make to meeting a range of housing needs within an overall rehousing strategy. Examples have been used to show how a transfer policy can address issues of housing preference, combat under-occupation, and create vacancies to meet other housing needs. However, again there may be tensions if transfers are encouraged at a cost of seeking to encourage stability in local communities.

The research emphasises the need for more detailed monitoring of local lettings schemes to see that outcomes are both fair and intended. This is an issue considered in more detail in Chapter 4 in relation to lettings in general and to fast-track approaches in particular.

Chapter 4:

The impact of lettings policies

4.1 Introduction

Chapters 2 and 3 have identified a wide range of different approaches being taken by local authorities and registered social landlords in respect of their letting and exclusion policies. Chapter 2 also noted the main areas of change in policies since the implementation of the Housing Act 1996. This chapter looks at the impact of allocation policies by examining the outcomes under different approaches and for different groups. In doing this, the chapter draws on local lettings statistics, information from each of the case study areas and responses to the random and innovation surveys. In particular, the chapter attempts to identify the impact of various approaches to lettings on the housing chances of homeless households and people in housing need.

4.2 Organisational perspectives

The impact of change

A note of caution needs to be flagged up here. The highest proportion of responses to all questions was that there had not been any change in factors such as the degree of choice for applicants or the length of time taken to be rehoused. In addition, as was noted by the national organisations, the level of demand will be a significant contextual factor in determining the speed of rehousing and degree of choice.

Respondents to the random survey were asked a number of questions that attempted to identify their perceptions of the ways in which access to social housing has changed over the two years prior to the survey. The responses are shown in Table 4.1. Nearly a third of respondents thought that their organisation's housing register was more open than previously, compared to just over 10 per cent thinking that their organisation's housing register was less open. Nearly a quarter of respondents thought that there was more choice for homeless households than previously, compared to just over 10 per cent thinking that there was less choice.

TABLE 4.1   **Perceptions of changes in access to social housing**

Question	More		Less		Same answer		Don't know /no		Total	
	No.	%	No.	%	No.	%	No.	%	No.	%
Is the housing register more or less open than two years ago?	22	34	7	11	28	43	8	12	65	100
Is there more or less choice for housing register applicants than two years ago?	21	32	17	26	23	35	4	6	65	100
Is there more or less choice for homeless households than two years ago?	15	23	7	11	35	54	8	12	65	100
Are homeless households rehoused in more, less or about the same amount of time as two years ago?	12	19	11	17	24	37	18	28	65	100
Is it more or less difficult to get a home, than two years ago, if you have children?	14	22	13	20	30	46	8	12	65	100
Is it more or less difficult to get a home than two years ago, if you do not have children?	15	23	20	31	22	34	8	12	65	100

Source: Random sample survey responses

Local lettings – judging success

Of 16 organisations responding to the innovation survey that had local lettings policies in place, just one stated that it considered that its local lettings policy had not met its objectives. Two organisations stated that they did not know whether their policies had met their objectives, while the remaining 13 considered that the objectives of their policies had been met.

This was despite a significant variation in the extent to which these policies were actually monitored and evaluated. A number of policies involved setting specific targets for lettings against which actual performance could be monitored. In one example, the proportion of black and minority ethnic households being rehoused had increased, which was one of the aims of the policy. Another way of measuring success was a reduced, or low, number of transfer requests or people moving out of tenancies to other tenures. Other 'success' factors which were identified were the creation of demand where little had existed, establishing a more positive image of the estate in the wider locality and people 'looking after' their properties.

Some respondents acknowledged that assessing the success of a local lettings policy was a subjective exercise. A number noted that any positive change in the area(s) where the policy applied was due to a range of factors, of which local lettings was only one. In one case, no evaluation or review of the policy had been carried out, but the respondent still considered that the policy had met its objectives.

4.3 Profiling the case studies

In the remainder of this chapter we have drawn upon different elements of our case study work in five organisations/areas to examine the impact of changes in lettings. However, before doing this it is important to look at the profile of the stock, the housing register and lettings in each of the five areas.

This must be seen against the national and regional background examined in section 1.2. Despite the decline in the scale of social housing, the level of lettings has been sustained and local authority housing registers show a continuing demand for social housing.

Tables 4.2 and 4.3 illustrate the profile of the local authority stock and housing registers in the five areas in which case studies were undertaken. In our RSL case studies, we have considered the HIP data from the local authorities in which more detailed case study analysis was carried out. In two areas (Rochdale and Sheffield) the local authorities are reporting relatively high levels of unpopular housing (significantly above both the national and regional averages), whereas in the other three areas the proportion of unpopular properties being reported is below the average.

In terms of numbers on the housing register, Lewisham's figures are broadly in line with the overall picture for London (slightly higher in 1998). Both Kensington and Chelsea and Sheffield report large numbers on their housing registers in relation to their stock. However, in Sheffield's case only a small proportion (15-16 per cent) are considered to be in need.

In terms of their profiles of lettings (Tables 4.4 and 4.5), in 1998 both London boroughs recorded a high proportion of new secure lettings to priority homeless households. Where authorities have made non-secure lettings (Sheffield in both years and Lewisham in 1999), virtually all of these have been to priority homeless people. However, outside of London (and non-secure tenancies) lettings to homeless households have been relatively low (though higher in Halton than either the national or regional average).

The tables also illustrate the proportions of RSL lettings made in each year in each area to priority homeless households, which are broadly in line with the patterns shown in Chapter 1, although there are quite significant differences between the two years in some cases.

The case studies

TABLE 4.2 Local authority stock, difficult-to-let stock and housing registers: five case study areas, 1998

Local authority	Stock	Difficult-to-let	Difficult-to-let as per cent of stock	Housing register total (exc. transfers)	Housing register as per cent of stock	Housing register in need (households wanting housing at current time)	Housing register in in need as as per cent of stock
Halton	7,811	464	6%	1,021	13%	1,021	13%
RB Kensington and Chelsea *	7,522	0	0%	7,527	100%	6,218	83%
LB Lewisham	33,532	No info.	-	13,922	42%	13,922	42%
Rochdale	17,368	4,802	28%	5,425	31%	3,269	19%
Sheffield	68,274	14,997	22%	54,389	80%	10,577	16%

Source: HIP data, DETR

* Common housing register

TABLE 4.3 Local authority stock, difficult-to-let stock and housing registers: five case study areas, 1999

Local authority	Stock	Difficult-to-let	Difficult-to-let as per cent of stock	Housing register total (exc. transfers)	Housing register as per cent of stock	Housing register in need (households wanting housing at current time)	Housing register in in need as as per cent of stock
Halton	7,722	231	3%	1,152	15%	1,152	15%
RB Kensington and Chelsea *	7,427	0	0%	7,671	103%	6,336	85%
LB Lewisham	32,835	0	0%	11,520	35%	11,520	35%
Rochdale	17,240	4,158	24%	3,582	21%	3,203	19%
Sheffield	66,864	18,459	27%	49,609	74%	9,783	15%

Source: HIP data, DETR

* Common housing register

TABLE 4.4   Lettings: five case study areas, 1997/98

Local authority	Lettings to new secure tenants	Priority homeless		Lettings to new tenants on a non-secure basis	Priority homeless		RSL lettings including nominations, exc. transfers	Priority homeless	
		No.	Per cent		No.	Per cent		No.	Per cent
Halton	480	102	21%	0	0	0%	920	29	3%
RB Kensington and Chelsea	372	236	63%	0	0	0%	645	170	26%
LB Lewisham	1,626	1,636	100%	89	0	0%	588	56	10%
Rochdale	2,630	147	6%	0	0	0%	860	10	12%
Sheffield	5,474	441	8%	665	637	96%	1,440	115	8%

Source: HIP data, DETR

TABLE 4.5   Lettings: five case study areas, 1998/99

Local authority	Lettings to new secure tenants	Priority homeless		Lettings to new tenants on a non-secure basis	Priority homeless		RSL lettings including nominations, exc. transfers	Priority homeless	
		No.	Per cent		No.	Per cent		No.	Per cent
Halton	407	63	15%	0	0	0%	901	31	3%
RB Kensington and Chelsea	120	0	0%	0	0	0%	663	154	23%
LB Lewisham	1,440	672	47%	103	103	100%	03	111	22%
Rochdale	2,569	169	7%	0	0	0%	622	8	1%
Sheffield	5,994	455	8%	751	730	97%	2,084	31	2%

Source: HIP data, DETR

In addition to the quantitative data, officers interviewed within the case study organisations were asked what they knew about customer perceptions of the rehousing process. The main concerns raised by officers were:

- despite the number of properties available due to low demand, the organisation was frequently not able to meet the aspirations of housing applicants in terms of location (Sheffield). The system could produce outcomes which were not equitable. For example, people with similar underlying needs could end up with a very different quality offer as perceived by both officers and applicants (Sheffield)

- frequently not being able to meet the needs of Asian families who often had very specific requirements, for example in terms of larger property in particular areas. One approach to addressing this was making block offers to a number of Asian families in the same road at the same time to try and ensure that they would not be isolated (Rochdale)

- most of the applicants nominated to Notting Hill Housing Trust by partner local authorities were only allowed one offer. The trust noted that this could result in people being rehoused in properties that they did not want and could lead to housing management problems and increased pressure on the transfer list.

4.4 The impact of specific changes and approaches

a)   CDS Housing: neighbourhood housing plans

The area chosen to undertake the application monitoring before and after a change in the lettings policy was Castlefield in Runcorn. The majority of the 650-plus homes on the estate are deck access two-bedroom flats initially designed for family living. A large part of the estate has seen major refurbishment and is maintained in a good condition.

Castlefield became a neighbourhood housing plan area in January 1999 because of falling demand and high turnover. The plans involve setting targets for households with various characteristics. Two samples of lettings were taken covering the periods July-September 1998 and July-September 1999. During the three-month period in 1998, 33 lettings were carried out, while 37 were carried out during the second period. The most significant differences in lettings between the two periods are summarised below.

There was a decrease, between the samples, in the number of applicants rehoused from the waiting list (62 per cent post-change as compared to 82 per cent pre-change). There were increases in the number of transfers (19 per cent, 6 per cent) and nominations (11 per cent, 0 per cent). The difference in the level of nominations is due to the availability of houses on Castlefield, as nominations are only sought for houses. There does not appear to be anything in the neighbourhood housing plan that would lead to the increase in transfers.

Characteristics of those rehoused

There were only minor differences in the profiles of households housed during the two periods. Broadly speaking, the age distribution of new tenants was similar for each sample, although there was a decrease in the proportion of lettings to women and an increase in lettings to men.

In terms of household type there was an increase in the proportion of single persons housed (particularly single men) and a decrease in the proportion of lone-parent households. There was also an increase in the proportion of tenants who had previously lived with family or friends and a decrease among households already holding tenancies, particularly in the private rented sector.

After the change in policy, two applicants who were classified as statutorily homeless were rehoused, compared to none in the sample before the change. This can be explained by an increase in nominations. The vast majority of households in both samples had local connections. The range of incomes remained broadly similar, despite efforts to attract more employed people.

A direct comparison could not be made between the two samples as to those able to sustain tenancies. However, of the pre-change sample almost two thirds were still tenants after at least 15 months, while almost 90 per cent of the post-change sample remained tenants after five months.

b)   Notting Hill Housing Trust: prioritising transfers

The pre- and post-change applicant sample was taken from two different estates in the Royal Borough of Kensington and Chelsea, one let in 1996, the second in 1999. Applicants for both developments came from the common housing register and Notting Hill Housing Trust's internal transfer list. The size of both samples was 40 lettings.

The Rootes estate (1996) is a traditional development of family-sized housing that was developed by Notting Hill Housing Trust with three other RSLs. Shaftesbury (1999) is a development of flats above a supermarket. It is primarily for single people and childless couples, although there is some family accommodation and part of the development comprises properties for shared ownership. The type of property allocated was 26 houses and 13 flats and one other unit on the Rootes estate and two houses and 38 flats on the Shaftesbury.

Rootes was let with nominations taken from the top of the common housing register for 75 per cent of lettings. Notting Hill Housing Trust stated that more selectivity was applied in letting the Shaftesbury estate. There was an intention to reduce the number of homeless households allocated to the Shaftesbury estate.

There was an increase between the samples in the proportion of transfer applicants rehoused. Notting Hill Housing Trust can negotiate with the Royal Borough of Kensington and Chelsea to house a greater proportion of transfer applicants on new estates, provided that the chain of vacancies which results produces a letting for a nomination. There was no record of the number of nominations rejected (if any), no details of nominees who were rejected for the development, and no reasons for rejection.

Characteristics of those rehoused

The noticeable changes in rehousing were the higher proportions of lettings to households with incomes in excess of £7,500 a year and the higher proportions of lettings to those who had previously held a tenancy in the Shaftesbury sample compared with the earlier lettings on the Rootes estate. There was also a small reduction in the proportion of lettings made to statutorily homeless households in the 1999 lettings. However, given the intention to reduce the proportion of lettings to households who were homeless on first letting of the Shaftesbury estate, this is unsurprising.

c)   Sheffield: fast-track rehousing route

In Sheffield a sample of rehousing cases was taken for one month in one relatively low demand area of the city. In an attempt to assess the impact of the fast-track rehousing route, comparisons were drawn between those rehoused through this route and general housing register and transfer applicants. During April 1999, 47 households were rehoused in this area, over half (26) via the general register, 13 via transfers, and just eight using the fast-track housing help desk. In general the differences between the three routes were fairly small. In all cases the majority of lettings were to single person households, with the majority of applicants being under 40 (although almost half the transfer cases rehoused were aged 60 or more). There were no homeless applicants rehoused in the area during the period, although we believe this is atypical. The only really noticeable differences in the pattern of lettings to applicants under the three different routes was that all those rehoused through the fast track route (and almost all general register applicants) were rehoused in flats and maisonettes, whereas those rehoused through transfers were more likely to be let a house. More surprisingly, there was no real evidence of the fast track route actually leading to people being rehoused more quickly.

4.5 Housing outcomes for applicants with different characteristics

In each case study organisation, a member of staff with a policy/management function and two members of staff involved in letting properties were asked to how they would treat ten different applicants. The cases are real, but names have been removed:

1   Couple with three children, evicted from a local authority tenancy six months prior to their application for rent arrears which resulted from difficulties in their relationship and temporary/unstable employment. Staying with friends sharing a two-bedroom house with another family with two children. One of the couple is suffering from anxiety and depression.

2   Single man aged 40 living in housing association property of which his mother was the sole tenant until she died four months prior to the application for rehousing. Housing association has started legal action to regain possession of the property, as he cannot succeed to the tenancy. Has long-standing depressive illness.

3   17-year-old woman living in a hostel on a licence agreement after being forced to leave home. She has her own room and bathroom but shares other facilities with other residents. Finding the situation difficult to cope with and has received warnings for aggressive/threatening behaviour. Wants to leave the hostel.

4   Lone parent with two children living in a shared ownership house. Unable to meet the shortfall in housing costs (rent and mortgage interest are being paid) and arrears are building up although the lender is not currently taking action. Divorced. Ex-partner was violent during marriage and is now being verbally abusive and sending hate mail. Needs to find alternative accommodation because of ex-partner's behaviour.

5   Couple with two children who have fled violence to live in the area where their parents live. Staying with family in a three-bedroom council house, six adults and two children altogether. Female applicant's health needs make it vital for her to live near family support.

6   Single man who has been sleeping rough for three months, previously in privately rented bedsit and before that in a hostel from which he states he was evicted following a drugs overdose by another resident which the staff team claimed had taken place in his bedroom. Registered with the probation service and awaiting treatment from a local addiction unit.

7   Young woman living in a privately rented bedsit. Three-year-old daughter living with her parents who have residency order because she did not have suitable accommodation. Had been made homeless

after being beaten by her father and then evicted from a private
tenancy on the grounds of nuisance. On the housing register of two
councils but suspended by one due to rent arrears on current tenancy.

8 Woman aged 50 who owns her own home out of the area. Came to live
with her daughter who has acute schizophrenia and daughter's three-
year-old son who live in two bedroom housing association flat in a high
demand area. Needs accommodation near to her daughter.

9 Woman aged 29 and six-month-old daughter living in rented
accommodation owned by a friend of her ex-partner. Has no tenancy
agreement although has lived there for five years. Ex-partner regularly
comes round uninvited and has a history of mental cruelty and
violence towards her. Has rent arrears of £700 with the council dating
back over five years.

10 Young man aged 27 with drug and alcohol problems, in care until 16
years of age. In and out of prison since age 17 and has never had a
settled home. Came to the area to visit a friend and would like to settle.
Staying at a friend's shared rented house and cannot stay there long.

The staff were asked to give information on each case including:

• **whether each applicant would be excluded or not**

• **what priority their application would be given**

• **how long it might take for them to be rehoused**

• **whether a referral to any other agency would be made**

• **whether support would be provided as well as housing**

• **what sort of choice each applicant would have in terms of the area in which they
would be rehoused**

• **what type of housing would be likely to be provided.**

Based on information received from four of the five case studies we have been able
to examine some of the likely different outcomes.

Two of the case study organisations reported that five of the ten applicants were
likely to be excluded from housing. Notting Hill indicated that applicant two was
likely to be excluded on age grounds, while applicant eight would not be likely to be
considered because she was a home owner. Rochdale suggested that applicants one
and nine would be likely to be excluded due to debt, and applicant six on account of
past behaviour.

The degree of choice offered under different lettings policies also varied quite
widely. Notting Hill suggested that applicants four, seven and nine were likely to
have a reasonable amount of choice, but all the others rather less. In all cases
applicants could expect to receive only one reasonable offer. Rochdale felt that all
but one (applicant four) of the seven applicants not excluded would be likely to have
a reasonable amount of choice over their rehousing, and in many cases would have

no limit on the number of offers they were likely to receive (particularly where this was via Selectahome). Applicant four, if accepted as priority homeless, would only receive one reasonable offer.

The situation in Sheffield was very similar, with all applicants expected to have a reasonable degree of choice as to where they could be rehoused. However, officers indicated that where applicants were likely to be accepted as homeless (cases two, three, four, six, nine, ten - and possibly five) they would be subject to only one reasonable offer. The authority also indicated that in a number of instances it would be likely to grant a temporary tenancy (applicants six, seven, and nine). In one case (applicant five), Sheffield indicated that the applicant would probably be rehoused through medical priority, which was seen as more effective than the homelessness channel.

In gathering this information we were sometimes able to discern differences within organisations between officers letting properties and those responsible for central monitoring. This was most marked in relation to CDS Housing.

4.6 Monitoring

A consistent conclusion from previous research has been that regular monitoring of the letting process and its outcomes is essential (see, for example, Griffiths et al, 1997). The Chartered Institute of Housing's housing management standards manual recommends monitoring: the volume of new applications; cancellations; offers; acceptances; refusals and the reasons for them; nominations made and accepted; accommodation secured from other landlords; by rehousing group. This should be broken down by ethnic origin, gender and disability and by the quality, size, type and location of properties compared with targets.

The case study local authorities and RSLs all have good organisation-wide monitoring systems in place. For example, Sheffield City Council carries out ethnic monitoring on an annual basis, allowing comparison of the proportion of lettings made via various access routes with the make-up of the housing register as shown in Table 4.6.

Table 4.6 Sheffield City Council waiting list and lettings by ethnic origin (percentage) 1997/98 and 1998/99

1997/98

	Waiting list (active)	Waiting list (suspended)*	Transfers	New Lettings to Statutory Homeless	New Tenancies	Total Permanent Lets
European	87%	53%	88%	83%	86%	86%
Black British	1.6%	0.9%	1%	1.5%	2%	1.7%
Pakistani	2.4%	0.8%	0.3%	1.8%	1%	0.8%
Caribbean	1%	0.8%	0.8%	0.7%	1%	0.9%

* 43% of suspended waiting list applicants' ethnic origin unknown 1998/99

1998/99

	Waiting list (active)	Waiting list (suspended)*	Transfers	New Lettings to Statutory Homeless	New Tenancies	Total Permanent Lets
European	88%	61%	88%	84%	86%	86%
Black British	1.5%	1%	1.1%	3.3%	2.7%	2.2%
Pakistani	2.4%	0.7%	0.4%	2.9%	1%	0.9%
Caribbean	0.8%	0.7%	0.7%	0.7%	0.8%	0.8%

* 35% of suspended waiting list applicants' ethnic origin unknown 1998/99

Given the increasing diversity of approaches and the use of local lettings policies, monitoring of the outcomes of the letting process needs to be carried out at an area/estate level as well as at an organisation-wide level. This is taking already place in some of the case study organisations. For example, Sheffield monitors the length of tenancy in accommodation which is let on a furnished basis.

The neighbourhood housing plan approach implemented by CDS Housing is supported by regular monitoring. This includes the number of starter tenancies created, those terminated at the end of 12 months, the extent and outcome of appeals, tenancy abandonments, starter tenancies transferred to assured tenancies, turnover rates and refusals, as well as information on numbers on the local waiting list.

At a more strategic level, the London Borough of Lewisham has developed a detailed analysis of changes in supply and demand, and how this has changed from one year to the next, with a view to informing policy responses. Thus it has noted that the number of lettings has declined year-on-year since 1995/96.

Table 4.7 Total lettings in Lewisham since 1995/96

Year	Number
1995/96	3,713
1996/97	3,352
1997/98	3,032
1998/99	2,369
1999/00 (April - Dec)	1,647 (projected 2,196 for whole year)

Explanations for this decline include: a fall in the number of tenants leaving the sector to buy in the private market; a reduction in RSL new-build; the impact of estate action and single regeneration budget programmes (with requirements for decants); an increase in right to buy sales; and the use of a small proportion of the council's permanent stock as temporary accommodation for asylum seekers.

However, alongside this downward trend in lettings, demand is increasing as the number of homeless acceptances has been growing (as is generally the case across London). Meanwhile, Home Office decisions on asylum seekers have been slow (and national arrangements for dispersal equally slow). The scale of the decant programme has grown considerably since 1997/98. In the first nine months of 1999/2000 some 42 per cent of lettings were made to priority homeless/asylum seekers (compared with 25 per cent in 1995/96), 35 per cent of lettings were to transfer applicants and just 23 per cent were to general waiting list applicants.

By analysing the ways in which the supply of properties has been 'spent' in the borough over recent years, broken down between transfers, waiting list and priority homeless, the authority has been able to take specific action to address the problems. Measures taken include nominating only priority homeless people to RSLs, seeking RSL vacancies above the agreed level for nominations, accessing private rented accommodation and seeking out-of-London accommodation for single asylum seekers. Lewisham has also used its strategic rehousing plan to develop longer term policies, including proposals to set up a targeted cash incentive scheme to release large homes, to build additional hostel accommodation, and to seek to discharge the council's homelessness duty via the private sector.

4.7 Conclusions

The random survey has shown that social landlords believe that access to social rented housing has changed since the introduction of the Housing Act 1996. Nearly a third thought their housing register was more open than previously, compared with just over 10 per cent who considered it more restrictive. Almost a quarter of social landlords thought there was more choice for households who were homeless, compared to just over 10 per cent who thought there was less. However, the highest proportion of social landlords felt there had been no change, either in the degree of choice or the time taken for rehousing. Clearly, levels of local demand are an important factor in determining both choice and the prospects for rehousing.

Where local lettings policies have been introduced, the majority of social landlords consider they have been meeting their objectives. However, several noted that this was often a subjective exercise. In many instances the degree of monitoring and evaluation of such schemes is very limited, making it difficult to determine the success or otherwise of these initiatives.

The research has sought to examine the impact of specific changes in approaches to lettings in a number of case study organisations. Whilst the number of lettings analysed has been small, and direct comparison has often been difficult, the available evidence suggests only marginal changes in the profiles of those housed. In areas of relatively low demand there is some evidence of increased lettings to single people and of applicants being more likely to be rehoused in their preferred area. However, in Sheffield, the introduction of a fast-track route does not seem to have led to applicants being rehoused more quickly. In the London example (Notting Hill), the evidence is of a higher proportion of first lettings to transfer applicants, and a small reduction in the allocations to homeless households, although the generation of vacancies by transfers may have given additional rehousing opportunities elsewhere for meeting priority housing need.

The use of anonymous cases has indicated the variation in the use of exclusions by different social landlords and the degree of housing choice to be offered. In particular, it reinforces our view of the need for more effective monitoring not only of the outcomes of lettings at a local level by social landlords, but also of how and why individual applicants are being excluded. Such policies and practices need to be accountable and subject to close monitoring and review.

This will enable the impact of local schemes on a wider area to be quantified. If this is not done, the danger is that people in need may be squeezed out of a number of localised schemes. Proper analysis is important in the context of neighbourhood renewal. Assessment of the impact of localised lettings policies on a wider area should be taken by local authorities as part of the development of homelessness prevention strategies and shared with all local landlords and local strategic partnerships.

Chapter 5:

Conclusions and recommendations

5.1 Conclusions

The research into social housing lettings has confirmed both the complexity of the process and the many different objectives which lie behind it. There are clear tensions between these different objectives. Most significantly, meeting the requirements of those in priority need may conflict with making sensitive lettings which address needs in a wider arena. At the same time, giving priority according to need may conflict with making best use of the stock and developing stable communities.

There are problems with the current system. For example, the use of multiple criteria for measuring different aspects of need may result in overly complex systems of needs assessment, and policies and practices which are not always easily understood. However, the evidence suggests that most social landlords are still seeking to prioritise lettings according to needs-based criteria.

The way lettings are organised varies considerably between social landlords. Our random sample of social landlords suggested a preponderance of centralised letting functions, although this was not mirrored either by the second-stage study of innovative practice or by the case studies, where decentralised systems were the norm. The balance of argument may be a fine one between achieving consistency across the organisation and adopting a more sensitive local approach. However, appropriate monitoring and audits of outcomes should enable a greater reliance on decentralised systems. In practice, the functions of a lettings system may represent a combination of central and local elements.

The study has examined the motivation for, and extent of, changes in lettings policies and practice since the Housing Act 1996. A number of new approaches have been identified. These include:

- changes in the extent to which exclusions and/or suspensions are used

- attempts to widen the range of applicants considered for rehousing

- speeding up the process and reducing bureaucracy

- changes in the scrutiny process for individual applicants

- applying different criteria to the assessment and prioritisation of applicants, with the aim of achieving a different mix of tenants

- relaxing eligibility criteria so that, as a matter of course, households can under-occupy property

- widening officer discretion in lettings.

Over half of the random sample of social landlords had made changes to the criteria for assessing housing need, in many cases to reflect the change of emphasis given in the Housing Act 1996 to the rehousing of homeless and vulnerable households. Almost half had either made changes to their policies on exclusions, or introduced such a policy for the first time. Nearly 20 per cent of landlords had changed the extent to which they use local lettings policies. A significant number indicated planned reviews to one or more elements of their lettings policies.

There were different motivations for change identified by national organisations and social landlords themselves. There were also differences between local authorities and RSLs. Local authorities were influenced primarily by the Housing Act 1996 changes, whereas RSLs were motivated by internal organisational change. The themes driving change included:

- **changing demand**

- **the competing interests of new and existing tenants**

- **the experience of communities when certain types of household have been rehoused**

- **wider debates about sustainable communities and the role of social housing.**

Local authorities and RSLs have applied a wide variety of exclusions, either from the housing register or from consideration for rehousing, although relatively few indicated a change in exclusions since the 1996 Act. RSLs more commonly excluded applicants than local authorities. The most common reported reasons for exclusions related to debt from current or former social housing tenancies and past anti-social behaviour. The research found that, where social landlords are excluding applicants from their housing registers, there is little monitoring of numbers or reasons.

Over half of the organisations reporting new approaches to lettings said they were trying to widen the range of potential applicants. In the random sample the proportion was over a third. In particular social landlords are using advertising and marketing approaches to attract groups such as those in employment. There are inevitably tensions between opening up access and meeting priority housing need, although these are less marked in areas where there is relatively low demand for social housing vacancies.

It is important to consider the scale of the many changes which have taken (and are taking) place. Findings from the random and innovation surveys show that a

significant minority of organisations have put new approaches in place across a
significant proportion of their stock.

Most social landlords which have introduced local lettings policies believe they are
meeting their objectives. However, several noted that this was often a subjective
exercise. In many cases the degree of monitoring and evaluation of schemes has
been limited, which makes it difficult to assess their strengths and weaknesses.

The research attempted to assess the impact of changes in lettings policies by
examining a small number of lettings both before and after the policy change in the
Housing Act 1996. The results suggest only marginal changes in the profiles of
households housed.

In areas of relatively low demand there is some evidence of a higher proportion of
lettings to single people. However, the introduction of a fast-track route to lettings
(in Sheffield) does not seem to lead to quicker rehousing. In our London example
(Notting Hill Housing Trust) a higher proportion of first lettings on new estates were
being made to transfer applications, with a small reduction in the allocations to
homeless households. This may have created additional housing opportunities
elsewhere for meeting priority need, although we cannot comment on their quality.

The study's use of anonymous case pen portraits identified wide variation in the use
of exclusions and in the degree of choice offered to different applicants. It reinforces
the need for more effective monitoring of both housing outcomes and exclusions at
a local level.

5.2 Recommendations

This research took place before the new policy direction set out in the Housing
Green Paper (DETR/DSS, 2000a) and 'The way forward for housing' (DETR/DSS,
2000c). However, it is vital to understand the trends it outlines if new policies and
practices are to be adopted successfully. This is of relevance not only to the
implementation of new legislation and a greater consumer focus, but also to the
development of the work of the Neighbourhood Renewal Unit. This report has
focused on the tensions between meeting individual need and the wider needs of a
neighbourhood. Reconciling these in practice will be key to the success of local
regeneration initiatives.

1) Transparency

Whatever detailed systems are in place, social housing lettings policies need to be
transparent to applicants. Clarity of policy and procedure is also important so that
officers, councillors and RSL board members can understand the process. Applicants
are entitled to clear information about:

- whether they are eligible for housing (in which areas, and of what type and size)

- how to apply and how the system works

- how priority is awarded

- how to appeal if they are not satisfied with how their application is handled

- what information they should expect to receive, and when.

2) Need

Lettings policies should continue to be based on needs-based criteria, although there is potential for a simpler way of assessing housing need. There may be scope for a core assessment which is common to all social landlords (as a national framework) and then for local discretion in determining other criteria. It is possible to envisage a number of priority groups for rehousing, which could comprise the following:

- statutorily homeless households

- non-statutorily homeless households (for example, homeless single people   not defined as being in priority need)

- young people defined as child in need by section 20 of the Children Act 1989

- households experiencing harassment and/or violence (including racial and sexual harassment and domestic violence)

- existing tenants under-occupying accommodation who wish to move to smaller homes

- asylum seekers entitled to accommodation and support

- households moving on from supported accommodation, including referrals from social services and voluntary groups

- households needing to be rehoused because of regeneration initiatives, or other statutory responsibilities (for example, demolition and closure orders, statutory overcrowding); management transfers and exceptional cases; and other households who are overcrowded, facing harassment or in unfit or poor quality accommodation.

Once the priority for each of these groups had been established, households could be offered housing on a date order basis. Other households who could show some evidence of housing need would then be considered in date order, and finally households not in housing need, again in date order. The Housing Green Paper (DETR/DSS, 2000a) argued for a more simplified banding system, but it is important to note that the housing needs of households are often highly complex and need to be reflected through appropriate criteria, particularly in areas of high housing need.

3) Choice

There is also a need to promote wider choice for both new and existing tenants, although it is acknowledged that the degree of choice which can be offered will vary according to local housing market conditions. This has been reiterated in ministerial statements and underpinned several measures in the Homes Bill. Choice and need within lettings policies can be compatible, although other current debates stress their incompatibility. Given the different contexts within which local authorities and RSLs are letting their housing, it is possible to set out a range of ways in which choice can be extended. The number of these which any individual organisation will be able to use will depend to a large extent on local housing markets. However, cultural change within organisations may be needed to enable a more consumer-driven approach. Choice can be extended by the following (not exhaustive) list of measures:

- providing clear, accurate and up-to-date information on properties, the surrounding environment, services provided by the landlord and facilities/services available from other organisations in local communities, including any regeneration initiatives. This could include use of information technology such as putting information on the internet

- using accompanied visits to help inform applicants about the property and surrounding environment. These can also serve as an opportunity to negotiate on a number of levels which may facilitate individual choice. For example, negotiation could take place about which repairs which will be carried out before the new tenant moves in, the provision of any decoration allowances/vouchers, any extra work which could be carried out by the landlord, or any extra time that may be allowed for the new tenant to move in, so that the tenant does not incur rent arrears at the start of the tenancy. Accompanied viewing has a clear role to play with respect to vulnerable tenants

- allowing applicants to state their area preferences more accurately, using definitions of areas which make sense to local communities. Other preferences could also be stated, including type and size of property and other facilities such as type of heating

- developing clear service standards in offer policies to reduce the number of inappropriate offers. The standards could include only making offers in an area of preference

- providing clear information to applicants about trade-offs and the implications of their choices, for example in terms of waiting time and availability of properties. IT systems need to be able to facilitate this

- using common housing registers can provide a choice of landlord and a larger number of potential vacancies

- on new developments, providing choice about individual properties and/or choice of neighbours

- using simultaneous offers of existing properties

- introducing flexible refusal policies or reducing, or abandoning, penalties for refusals of offers

- relaxing eligibility rules criteria so that households can get access to properties larger than their 'need'.

There is also a need to move towards greater equity of choice across different access routes. If equity is not attainable, then perhaps there is scope for an approach which guarantees that all offers will meet certain criteria such as being in one of an applicant's stated areas of preference. This will have implications for time spent in temporary accommodation, but if we are serious about extending choice then a reasonably fair approach has to be applied. Otherwise, homeless households will lose out and end up concentrated in the least popular areas as has happened in the past.

4)   Exclusions

The research has shown wide variation in the use of exclusions by social landlords. While there may be a case for exclusion in certain circumstances, the use of 'blanket' exclusions from the register of particular groups is not appropriate. This has been recognised by the Government in its proposals to remove landlords' scope to impose blanket restrictions (DETR/DSS, 2000c). However, there is also a need for closer monitoring of the use of exclusions and suspensions and clear guidance to applicants as to how these can be removed.

5)   Monitoring

In general there needs to be a greater emphasis on monitoring of lettings to prevent unfairness and unwanted outcomes. This can also be highly beneficial in developing policy responses to problems of mismatch between housing supply and demand.

The results of this monitoring are one of the key sources of information required when an individual housing organisation undertakes a major review of its lettings policy and practice. When carrying out such reviews, local authorities and RSLs need to test out proposed policy changes, in particular by identifying any 'winners' and 'losers' in terms of priority for rehousing. Given the requirements of best value, they will also need to consult with stakeholders including existing tenants, applicants to the general waiting list, homeless people and transfer applicants, as well as councillors or RSL board members, staff, partner organisations such as other social landlords working in the area, statutory bodies such as probation and social services and referral agencies.

6)   Transfers

There is a strong argument in favour of a greater emphasis on a strategic approach to lettings which recognises the potential for using transfers both to satisfy the needs and preferences of existing tenants wishing to move and to create vacancies which can be used to meet the needs of general applicants in priority need. This might include a requirement on local authorities to prepare annual lettings plans. There is also scope for the further encouragement of common housing registers.

7) Market conditions

Lettings policies (and local lettings policies, in respect of specific areas, estates, or blocks of property) need to be based upon an effective local analysis of housing market conditions. This needs to take account of the likely supply of and demand for social housing from different groups, given other housing opportunities, as well as broader national policies and directives.

5.3 Conclusion

Lettings policies that include factors other than housing need should only be initiated in the full knowledge of the impact they will have on all groups involved. While there may be scope for legislative change and administrative reform, there remains a need for continued flexibility and autonomy at a local level. It should also be recognised that changes in policies on access and lettings can only provide part of a solution to the problems of meeting priority need, tackling social exclusion and building sustainable local communities.

There may be scope for further guidance on who should be able to gain access to social rented housing and how applicants should be prioritised, but there remains a need for continued flexibility and autonomy at a local level. The research findings also suggest a need for continuing caution as to what can be achieved through lettings policies and practices to address what are often deep-seated problems, whether of acute housing need or declining demand for social housing.

Appendix 1:

Research methodologies

Stage 1: Telephone survey methodology

The local authorities were grouped initially by type of authority (inner London, outer London, metropolitan district, unitary, other districts, LSVT authorities). The districts were further split by region, based upon the Office of National Statistics (ONS) standard regions. A random sample was then taken from each of the resulting groups, proportionate to their scale (as a percentage of all local authorities in that group) and the size of the sample required.

The sample of RSLs was drawn from the Housing Corporation's 1998 register of social landlords, considering all those with 500 homes or more in management. RSLs which had been established as part of a voluntary transfer were excluded, since they had already been sampled as a category of local authorities. The sample was further stratified by size:

- **RSLs with 4,000 or more homes**
- **RSLs with 500-4,000 homes, grouped by Housing Corporation region**

Again, a random sample was taken from each of the resulting groups, proportionate to their size (in terms of all RSLs) and the size of sample required.

From the 82 organisations approached we completed stage one telephone interviews with 65, a response rate of 79 per cent, in summer 1999. We were either unable to contact the remaining 17 or they were unwilling to participate. Out of the 65 organisations where telephone interviews were completed, 44 provided further information and documentation related to their letting policies. In general, responses were in line with the overall profile of local authorities and RSLs by type and region. However, respondent local authorities were slightly over-represented in the South East and under-represented in relation to stock transfer authorities. RSL respondents were over-represented in London but under-represented in the West Midlands.

The questionnaire for the first stage telephone survey was organised under four main headings:

- general approach – operation of the housing register, access, criteria for needs assessment, offers and refusals, and joint working between local authorities and RSLs

- local lettings (objectives of local lettings policies operation in different areas/on different estates, details of policies in places, differences from standard approach to allocations) criteria taking account of role of tenants, monitoring and evaluation

- changes in organisations' lettings policies since the Housing Act 1996 (reasons for change, timing of change, details of change)

- interviewees' views of change (register more or less 'open', more or less difficult to obtain rehousing, additional choice for applicants and more or less time taken to rehouse?).

Stage 2: Telephone survey methodology

A second stage telephone survey was conducted in summer 1999 with 28 additional social landlords. The stage two respondents were identified either through stage one contact, via the Chartered Institute of Housing's good practice unit (GPU) or from the housing press.

The results of the stage two interviews, together with those local authorities and RSLs where new approaches to lettings had been identified from the stage one survey, were used to develop a typology of lettings and exclusions. In particular this covered whether:

- the motive for change was proactive or reactive

- the approach was applied to the whole of the stock, was area-based or property-based

- the approach was applied indefinitely or was time-limited;

- a more or less exclusionary approach was being taken

- the general policy on exclusions was being adhered to or by-passed at the local level

- there was increased or decreased vetting of applicants

- more or less officer discretion was involved.

The typology was used to select five local case studies for more detailed examination, although the identity of the case studies was also determined by a desire to ensure a mix of organisation type (local authorities/RSLs), a geographical spread, (with consideration of different levels of demand for social housing), and organisations that carried out monitoring of lettings to a reasonable standard.

Appendix 2:

Case studies

Five organisations were selected for more detailed investigation. This stage of the research was carried out in late 1999/early 2000.

CDS Housing

CDS Housing is an RSL which operates in the North West of England, with its highest concentrations of properties in Liverpool (3572) and Halton in Cheshire (843). It has 4,825 properties in management, with a further 157 units managed on its behalf by others, including tenant management organisations (TMOs). The housing management function is undertaken from three area offices serving Liverpool, Halton and the dispersed areas (Knowsley, Sefton and Wirral).

The organisation is experiencing relatively low demand for some of its stock, the inability of local authorities to provide nominations to vacancies, and relatively high turnover of tenancies. While its lettings policy prioritises housing need, it is developing more flexible policies where the supply of vacancies exceeds demand, and has been marketing properties, seeking to attract applications from a wider cross-section of the community. CDS has also implemented two neighbourhood housing plans (NHPs), where additional points are awarded for certain non-needs based criteria. The intention is to increase the demand for vacancies, reduce turnover of tenancies, and halt the decline in two specific neighbourhoods, one in Liverpool 8 and the other in Runcorn.

London Borough of Lewisham

Lewisham is an inner London authority situated to the south of the River Thames. It has a housing stock of about 110,000 homes, of which over 32,000 are in council ownership (almost 30 per cent of the stock). There are a further 7,350 homes provided by RSLs. Despite a relatively large stock of social rented housing, at the time of the study there were more than 19,000 households on the borough's rehousing register, over 11,500 on the general waiting/priority homeless list, and more than 7,500 existing council tenants seeking to transfer. While demand has grown since 1993/94, lettings are down from over 3,000 each year to about 2,400 per year, partly because the number of tenants leaving to buy has fallen as house prices have increased. The situation has been exacerbated by increased numbers of priority homeless households and a commitment to rehouse existing tenants as part of estate regeneration programmes. In order to address these pressures, and to prevent the use of bed and breakfast hotels, the council is using voids for temporary accommodation for families, encouraging those homeless households who are staying with family and friends to remain there, discharging homelessness duties via the RSL and private sectors, and seeking nominations above and beyond agreed levels.

There are enormous rehousing pressures within the borough, and the council gives priority to those with no permanent or secure housing, families, households containing vulnerable people and existing tenants with urgent transfer needs, or where rehousing would release much needed accommodation elsewhere. As part of an overall lettings strategy there are also policies to encourage transfers where this will help to make more effective use of the housing stock.

Notting Hill Housing Trust

Notting Hill Housing Trust (NHHT) is a regional RSL based in the west of London. It has a stock of 12,900 properties, the majority of which are in the London boroughs of Hammersmith and Fulham (over 4,000 properties) and Kensington and Chelsea (over 3,300). The remaining properties are located in a further nine inner and outer boroughs.

London (and in particular west London) has relatively high housing need, with high levels of demand for accommodation in the social rented sector. The main aim of the Trust is to provide rented housing for those on low incomes or occupying inadequate housing. Whilst this continues to be the central focus of the Trust's work, in recent years it has supplemented and broadened its outlook. Its capacity to address needs in its traditional inner London locations have become more restricted. In the light of high land costs, and particularly because of a lack of suitable sites, NHHT's ability to develop new housing in inner London has diminished, and shifted to outer boroughs, in particular Ealing and Hillingdon.

At the same time the Trust has sought to address social polarisation on its estates, through the active promotion of mixed communities. Complementing this has been a consideration of wider issues affecting households' housing needs, including the relationship between housing markets, local economies and local communities. The Trust's letting policy has acknowledged the relationship between the housing market and the local economy, supports the labour force needs of local communities, looks at the wider context of household's housing need (as well as their need for shelter), and actively plans for mixed communities to decrease social polarisation.

Rochdale Metropolitan Borough Council

The council has a total housing stock of some 17,000 homes and an annual turnover of around 3,000 properties. It has approximately 4,000 applicants for rehousing. However, around half of these are registered for 'future' rehousing or are not under active consideration, due to outstanding housing debt. In many parts of the borough there is an over-supply of social housing and difficulties in letting (not restricted to the local authority). There is also a reasonably large private rented sector competing with social landlords. The hope is that people will 'rediscover' the council sector. Overall, the local authority void rate is 2.6 per cent, although this is higher in parts of the borough, for example North Rochdale, which has large swathes of unpopular flatted accommodation. Rochdale is in economic decline, with a drift of population to more prosperous areas of Greater Manchester, and council housing's image has declined, such that it has become the 'tenure of last resort'.

To help overcome its very fundamental problems the council has introduced a fast-track rehousing service, Selectahome. This scheme (introduced in October 1998) is already accounting for some 80-90 lettings per month; around a third of all lettings. It is considered in more detail in Chapter 2.

Sheffield City Council

Although Sheffield has not experienced the loss of population faced by some northern cities, the local authority is facing low demand for many of its properties (18,500 out of 65,000 are judged to be difficult to let). There is evidence of an over-supply of social rented housing, a wide range of other housing options (relatively low-cost owner-occupation and opportunities in the private rented sector), and evidence of increasing polarisation within the city, with the west and south thriving while the north and east are in decline.

A wide range of initiatives has been put in place in response to changes in demand. This includes a help desk whose staff facilitate a fast-track route into local authority accommodation as well as carrying out extensive marketing and publicity for council homes. The local authority considers that there are now several parts of the city (predominantly council housing areas) which have reached the point where only a radical transformation of the social and physical fabric is going to prevent mass abandonment, persuade economically active residents to stay, and attract outsiders. Research undertaken by the council has shown that a significant reduction in the size of the social rented sector is needed if the problem of falling demand is not to become even more acute. The city established a 'Future of council housing' project (1999) to take action to achieve a housing stock of the size, quality and type, in the locations and at a cost, which meets the aspirations and needs of future residents and of which the city can be proud.

The case study approach

In each case study organisation we have sought to use four different, yet complementary, approaches to assess the impact of different allocation policies at a local level. These were:

- semi-structured face-to-face (and, where appropriate, supplementary telephone) interviews with key officers within each of the case study organisations, as well as some of the main agencies providing or accepting nominations/referrals. These interviews examined barriers to access, rehousing priorities, policies on transfers, exchanges, nominations and referrals, arrangements for rehousing homeless applicants, policies on offers and refusals, issues of choice and equity, and the monitoring of allocations decisions and outcomes

- the organisation's own monitoring data on applications, lettings, refusals etc

- the collection of data on a small cohort of applicants re-housed in the case study area, focusing on outcomes before and after a change in the lettings system. However, this information was only collected in three of the case studies, and it has proved extremely difficult at a local level to assess the impact of changes in letting policies and procedures as to whether some households have received enhanced priority whilst others may have had to wait longer for permanent housing. It is extremely difficult to look at specific estates or areas in isolation from wider housing markets and other factors which may have shaped either landlords' decisions or applicants' choice. More detailed district-wide longitudinal analysis may be appropriate in the future.

- a small number of anonymised real applications for rehousing in order to test these against local letting policies with both policy officers and front-line housing staff.

Bibliography

Annual Digest of CORE data (2000), University of St Andrews and Dundee.

Audit Commission (1992) Developing local authority housing strategies, HMSO, London.

Bines W, Kemp, P, Pleace N and Radley C (1993) Managing social housing: a study of landlord performance, HMSO, London.

Bramley G, Third H and Pawson H (2000) Low demand housing and unpopular neighbourhoods, Department of Environment, Transport and the Regions, London.

CHAC (1949) Selection of tenants, HMSO, London.

CHAC (1969) Council housing purposes, procedures and priorities, HMSO, London.

Chartered Institute of Housing (1996) Allocations and homelessness: the new framework, Chartered Institute of Housing, Coventry.

Cole I, Gidley G, Ritchie C, Simpson D and Wishart B (1996) Creating communities or welfare housing? a study of new housing association developments in Yorkshire and Humberside, Chartered Institute of Housing, Coventry.

Cole I, Kane S and Robinson D (1999) Changing demand, changing neighbourhoods: the response of social landlords, CRESR, Sheffield Hallam University.

Department of the Environment (1978) Allocation of council housing, Housing Services Advisory Group, London.

Department of the Environment (1980) An investigation of difficult to let housing, volume 1: general findings, Housing Development Directorate Occasional Paper 3/80, London.

Department of Environment, Transport and the Regions (1999a) Code of guidance for local authorities on the allocation of accommodation and homelessness Parts VI and VII of the Housing Act 1996 - consultation draft, DETR, London.

Department of Environment, Transport and the Regions (1999b) National Strategy for Neighbourhood Renewal report of policy action team 5 on housing management, DETR, London.

Department of Environment, Transport and the Regions (1999c) Housing investment programme (HIP) 1999 guidance notes for local authorities,
DETR, London.

Department of Environment, Transport and the Regions (1999d) National Strategy for Neighbourhood Renewal report of policy action team 7: unpopular housing, DETR, London.

Department of Environment, Transport and the Regions/ Department of Social Security (2000a) Quality and choice: a decent home for all, DETR/DSS, London.

Department of Environment, Transport and the Regions (2000b)
Homelessness statistics.

Department of Environment, Transport and the Regions/ Department of Social Security (2000c) The way forward for housing, DETR/DSS, London.

Forrest, R (2000) 'What constitutes a "balanced" community?' in Social exclusion and housing, Anderson I and Sim D (eds), Chartered Institute of Housing, Coventry, pp 207-219.

Glennester H and Turner T (1993) Estate based housing management: an evaluation, HMSO, London.

Griffiths M, Parker J, Smith R, Stirling T and Trott T (1996) Community lettings: local allocations policies in practice, YPS for Joseph Rowntree Foundation, York

Griffiths M, Parker J, Smith R and Stirling T (1997) Local authority housing allocations: systems, policies and procedures, DETR, London.

Holmans A and Simpson M (1999) Low demand: separating fact from fiction, Chartered Institute of Housing, Coventry.

Housing Corporation (1999) Addendum 4 to the social housing standards for general and supported housing: anti-social behaviour, Housing Corporation, London.

Institute of Housing (1990) Housing Allocations, IoH, Coventry.

Kleinman M, Aulakh S, Holmans A, Morrison N, Whitehead C and Woodrow J (1999) No excuse not to build, Shelter, London.

Lemos G and Goodby G (1999) A new spirit of community, Lemos and Crane/Manningham Housing Association, London and Bradford.

Local Government Association (1999) Report of the LGA allocations and homelessness task group, 488/99, LGA, London.

Maclennan D and Kay H (1994) Moving on, crossing divides, HMSO, London.

Murie A, Nevin B and Leather P (1998) Changing demand and unpopular housing, Housing Corporation, London.

Page D (1993) Building for communities, Joseph Rowntree Foundation,York.

Page D (1994) Developing communities, Sutton Hastoe Housing Association, Teddington.

Parker J, Smith R and Williams P (1992) Access, allocations and nominations: the role of housing associations, HMSO, London.

Pawson H (1998) Local authority stock turnover in the 1990s, Joseph Rowntree Foundation Findings 058, York.

Pawson H, Bramley G (2000) 'Would you live here?' ROOF, July/August 2000, Shelter, London

Pawson H, Kearns A, Keoghan M, Malcolm J and Morgan J (1997) Managing voids and difficult-to-let property, Housing Corporation, London.

Wilcox S (1999) Housing finance review 1999/2000, Chartered Institute of Housing and Council of Mortgage Lenders, Coventry and London.

Young M and Lemos G (1997) The communities we have lost and can regain, Lemos and Crane, London.